The People vs. Presidential War

Compiled and edited by
John M. Wells
with Maria Wilhelm

Foreword by
Senator J. William Fullbright

The People vs. Presidential War

The Dunellen Company, Inc., New York

International Standard Book Number 0-8424-0024-9.

Library of Congress Catalogue Card Number 74-136252.

Printed in the United States of America.

To the memory of
Jim Shea

Contents

Photographs

Contributors

Lawrence Adler—Boston lawyer living in Lexington, Massachusetts.

Jack H. Backman—Massachusetts State Representative, Vice Chairman of the Massachusetts Joint Judiciary Committee of the Legislature.

David M. Bartley—Speaker, Massachusetts House of Representatives.

John A. Businger—Administrative and Legislative Assistant to Representative H. James Shea, Jr.

Kenneth D. Campbell—Political reporter, the *Boston Globe.*

Richard Cauchi—Executive Secretary, Citizens for Participation Politics.

Maurice A. Donahue—Massachusetts Senate President.

John Dixon Elder—State Chairman (Massachusetts), Citizens for Participation Politics.

Richard Gaines—Legislative Reporter, United Press International, Boston.

Lee Goldstein—Teacher of Social Sciences in the Saugus, Massachusetts, High School.

Ernest Gruening—Former United States Senator from Alaska.

Fred King—Lab Instructor, Physics Department, Harvard University.

Elizabeth Latzer—Former writer for the *Newsletter* of the Science Action Coordinating Committee, M.I.T.

David Lustig—Contributing editor of the *Phoenix,* a Boston weekly news magazine.

Kenneth P. O'Donnell—1970 Democratic candidate for Governor, Massachusetts; former aide to President Kennedy.

Nicholas Peck—College student and correspondent for the *Boston Globe*.

Robin A. Remington—Research Associate, M.I.T. Center for International Studies.

Francis W. Sargent—Governor of Massachusetts.

Sharon Scofield—Housewife from Boston.

Mary Ann Seitz—Lexington housewife and coordinator of lobbying activities for the Shea-Wells Bill.

Daniel Small—Student in Lexington, Massachusetts, High School.

Robert L. Turner—Assistant City Editor, the *Boston Globe*.

Lawrence Velvel—Professor of Constitutional Law at the University of Kansas.

Joseph Ward—Chairman, Joint Judiciary Committee, Massachusetts General Court.

Jane Webb—Former Executive Secretary of PAX (Massachusetts Political Action for Peace).

Reverend John M. Wells—Minister of First Parish Church, Lexington, Massachusetts.

Charles L. Whipple—Editor of the Editorial Page, the *Boston Globe*.

Elizabeth and Stillman Williams—Lexington residents and members of the First Parish Church.

Foreword

Politics is the practical exercise of the art of self-government, and somebody must attend to it if we are to have self-government; somebody must study it, and learn the art, and exercise patience and sympathy and skill to bring the multitude of opinions and wishes of self-governing people into such order that some prevailing opinion may be expressed and peaceably accepted. Otherwise, confusion will result either in dictatorship or anarchy. The principal ground of reproach against any American citizen should be that he is not a politician. Everyone ought to be, as Lincoln was.

—Elihu Root
Speech presenting statue of
Lincoln to the British people
July 28, 1920.

The statement quoted above was pertinent when Elihu Root made it in 1920. It is essential today. The founding fathers of our Republic were well aware of the difference between being subjects and being citizens. They were British subjects. They became, as a result of the American Revolution, and the subsequent great experiment in self-government, citizens. Each American citizen, to protect his citizenship from eroding into a symbol rather than reality, must be constantly alert and ever-aware of what is happening at all levels of government.

American democratic institutions are only as valid as they are cherished and challenged by the American people. The framers of the U.S. Constitution carefully and meticulously sought to safeguard citizenship by establishing the system of checks and balances between the three branches of the federal government and the power residing within the individual states. There never was an intention for ultimate power to reside in the states, in the federal legislature, in the federal judiciary, or in the office of the president.

During the past several years there has been a drift of power at the federal level toward the chief executive. The possibility of thermonuclear war has raised a question of the need for greater discretion for the President to make war than is provided by the Constitution. But, has this danger negated the appropriate power that should reside in the Congress of the United States?

This is the very question raised by the Commonwealth of Massachusetts in its recently enacted statute questioning the constitutionality of the war in Vietnam. Has the drift in federal power now gone so far as to give the chief executive the ultimate power of taking this nation to war on his own initiative and keeping this nation in a prolonged military engagement without the specific and clear approval of the Congress of the United States?

The people of Massachusetts acted to resolve this question. Under a provision of their constitution, written in 1780 under the leadership of John Adams, a citizen can petition the General Court (the legislature) of Massachusetts for the enactment of legislation. This provision was acted upon by a minister, who is a former lawyer. A bill was drafted. It was taken by a sensitive and concerned freshman state representative and brought before the appropriate state legislative committee. It was nurtured and cultivated by a college professor. It was carried to the public by editors, newsmen, TV and radio broadcasters. It was debated thoroughly, in committee chambers and on the floor of the House and Senate. It was an appropriate and proper channel for the citizens of Massachusetts to be heard. And, indeed, they were heard. The question of the rights guaranteed by the federal Constitution should be the concern of all citizens and of all elected representatives. The enactment of the Shea-Wells Bill by the Massachusetts legislature was democracy in action; young people, older people, college students, university professors, housewives, gold-star mothers, and veterans joined together in being politicians in the best sense.

The war in Indo-China continues. The Massachusetts act has not ended the war. It has, however, brought to the attention of the entire nation and of the Congress of the United States a frightening prospect. Under present conditions, the President has exercized war-making power without the declaration by Congress as required in Article 1, Section 8 of the U. S. constitution.

It is now time for all Americans to become involved in this issue. The citizens of Massachusetts have led the way by acting as citizen politicians. The story of the enactment of this legislation is a fascinating recount of the democratic process in the best tradition. It is told by those who were the actors in this exciting drama. It is original source material by those who were there.

The hope of American democracy lies in such action. The Supreme Court may rule one way or the other. That is now the Court's responsibility. But, the action by caring citizens taking their concerns out of the streets into the halls of the legislature will stand as a continuing example of democracy at its best. The arguments were heard. The issue was joined. The majority won. Neither dictatorship nor anarchy can prevail in such a climate.

J. W. Fulbright
United States Senator
1970

Acknowledgments

I am indebted first of all to my wife, Rollene, whose enthusiasm and patience supported us both through forty-eight-hour days. Mrs. Jan Molloy, my secretary, was of invaluable assistance in making order out of incipient chaos during those busy days before Governor Sargent signed our bill into law. Nor could we have succeeded without the unstinting help of Mrs. Mary Ann Seitz, who coordinated the myriad activities of all who have contributed to this book, and many more.

And finally, I want to express my heartfelt thanks to the members of First Parish Church, whose devotion to freedom and the rights of man went far to make the Bill a reality.

1   The Little Pebble Cast

Charles L. Whipple

In his last speech to the Massachusetts House of Representatives, Rep. H. James Shea, Jr. was talking about the divisiveness of American society. "This whole breakdown," he said, "began with the assassination of John F. Kennedy."

"Whether you like it or not," he told his colleagues, just six days after the invasion of Cambodia, "I'm the only member of the Establishment talking with these groups who are so anti-Establishment. I'm just trying to keep society together in my humble way."

A few days later he was dead, and by his own hand. And a *Globe* reporter, Kenneth D. Campbell, who remembered how Shea had helped keep a demonstration at the State House peaceful after the Kent State killings, paid him this homage: " The kids to whom he had talked wrote his obituary with a can of spray paint on the base of a statue opposite the State House: 'Shea—He Lives.' "

And, quite apart from the reference to Che Guevara, in a larger sense indeed he does.

As the *Globe* said editorially on the day of his funeral, "The short life of this thirty-year-old lawmaker will be given still more meaning if his work is continued by others who believe in his kind of practical action within the law. The soul of Jim Shea, like that of John Brown, can still go marching on."

As this is written, the state legislation that bears Shea's name, intended to test the constitutionality of the draft for a foreign war when Congress has not declared that such a war exists, appears headed for a test before the United States Supreme Court. It has come a long way since it was filed as a bill and given almost no chance of passage.

The *Boston Globe* was both fortunate and happy to help it along some. It was for us an easy and natural thing to do, because the bill was so consistent with our editorial policy. We had been printing editorials pointing out the folly of the war in Vietnam since the middle of 1965, when President Lyndon B. Johnson began in earnest to heighten the war effort ("escalate," I am told, is not really a word, but then, there are those these days who say an invasion is not really an invasion).

And so, on January 30, 1970, the *Globe* called attention to the Shea bill, and we added, "If the spirit of Thoreau should so move the Legislature to pass it, this little pebble cast on the water could make some mighty big waves!"

We followed that with an editorial on March 16 praising 116 lawmakers for voting initial approval of the bill, and again March 18 after final House passage. We said then:

> Passage of the bill should not embarrass Governor Sargent, who commendably made clear his doubts about the war last October 15 in Lexington. Nor should it embarrass President Nixon for whom, as for his predecessor, the legality of the war so far has not been tested in the courts despite the grave doubts of many in Congress and among the citizenry.
> The House has spoken, and spoken well. The Senate and Governor Sargent ought to do likewise. If they do, Daniel Webster's famous words—"Massachusetts, there she stands!"—will have assumed new meaning, and the nation will have some chance of being relieved at last, as far as draftees are concerned, of the oppressive burden of the most unpopular war in its history.

With Senate passage assured, the *Globe* on April 1 urged that the bill be signed by Governor Francis W. Sargent, who had discussed the matter at the White House. We recalled the governor's words on October 15, 1969, at the Lexington peace demonstration, when he said of the people of Vietnam: "It is their country. It is their war. It is not our country. It is not our war."

Under the heading, "The Whole Country Is Watching," the *Globe* said, "The governor spoke for the people then, and he would speak for the people now by approving the bill. Let Massachusetts once again, as she did in her proudest days, show the nation the way!"

The governor signed the bill the next day, and the *Globe* praised all concerned on April 3. It recalled its own words about the small pebble possibly making "some mighty big waves" and concluded, "Now let it make them."

Since then, the Attorney General of Massachusetts, Robert Quinn, has filed his suit in behalf of the Commonwealth. It is much too early for any self-congratulation. The really big waves are still to be made. That will be up to the highest court in the land.

But whichever way that court decides—if indeed it does decide— something has been started in Massachusetts by Rev. John M. Wells and Jim Shea and by all those others who helped them that I believe will have profound significance for historians. It is a matter of considerable pride to us at the *Boston Globe* that we were able to play some small part in it all.

2   The Minister's Story

Reverend John M. Wells

During the past year, many people have asked me why I drafted and filed in the Commonwealth of Massachusetts legislation designed to test the constitutionality of the Vietnam war. The story is a long one.

First of all, I am an attorney—Emory University, Atlanta, Georgia, 1952. The war in Korea was still in progress when I went to law school, and because I needed money I had joined an army reserve outfit. We met on Thursday nights and played at being soldier. After I got my degree, I joined the Air Force as a judge advocate—a lawyer in the government's service. This way, I thought, I could follow my profession and serve my country. Otis Air Force Base, Dobbins, then Africa enlarged my heretofore provincial view of my country and the world.

I had been an ardent student of constitutional law while I was in law school. I love the concept of the protection given to the citizens of the United States under the Constitution. It bothered me when the American military forces who were stationed out of their country were denied their constitutional rights. Yet, I came to grips with the fact that when a person was off duty in the military, he was the same as anyone else visiting a foreign country; and that a nation should have the right to determine within its own borders what its own provisions of law are and what the penalties for violations should be. I realized that a nation's constitutional prerogatives must be protected from anyone—

even from people who were coming there as "protectors," as we were labeled in those days in Morocco, Greece, Turkey, Italy, and elsewhere within the Mediterranean area where I had the opportunity to travel.

Back in Georgia, my tour of duty terminated, I was confronted with another constitutional problem—racism. I was a liberal in a state that had not yet awakened to its responsibility to insure the constitutional rights of all its citizens. I made the agonizing decision to leave the South and return to the military, where I could believe as I wanted to believe, as long as I did my duty. And my "duty" changed my direction. (The military has never been my enemy. I wanted to call the Shea-Wells Bill the G.I. Rights Bill, because that, basically, is what it is.)

When I reported for duty in the Air Force again, this time to the Pentagon, I was assigned to the office of the Assistant Secretary of Defense for Manpower. In 1955 the Congress of the United States had enacted certain suggested legislation about voting. I use that peculiar terminology "suggested legislation" because the Congress had passed legislation suggesting to the states that they reform and revise their absentee voting laws to make it possible for persons in the armed forces to vote by an absentee ballot in an efficient way. We have two and one half to three million people within the military plus their wives and dependents, a larger number of people voting by absentee ballot than any other category of people, and they are scattered in numerous nations across the globe. Congress had seen fit to ask the states to revise their absentee registration and voting procedures to enable these people, who were called upon to defend the right to vote, to be enabled to vote.

I was given the task of working with the absentee voting program, which was known as the Federal Voting Assistance Program and located in the Office of the Secretary of Defense. Within a period of five months after my assignment, I was the only attorney left in the Federal Voting Assistance Program and began the very interesting and sometimes difficult task of working with state governments across the union. From 1957 to 1961 this was my full-time employment. I worked with every state in their administrative procedures pertaining to absentee registration and voting; and I worked with some thirty-eight state legislatures in the drafting and working through their legislatures of various amendments and procedures to provide voting processes for members of the armed forces, their wives and dependents, and other federal employees. I came intimately in touch with the very delicate relationship between the federal power under the Constitution and the

6

state power under the various state constitutions and legislative procedures.

My second profession is the ministry. Even before I became a lawyer, I had studied for the Methodist ministry at Duke University, where I had received my A.B. degree in 1947. Again in 1957, I entered Emory University Theological School, but traditional Christianity was not for me. I discovered Unitarian-Universalism during my tour of duty in Washington, D.C., and left the Air Force to study for the ministry at St. Lawrence University and Howard University. My quest has always been a religious one; my goal in government has been to bring the symbolic kingdom of God into reality here and now.

I was called to be minister of Mt. Vernon Unitarian Church in Alexandria, Virginia. I worked for civil rights; I went to Selma; I was one of the ministers to meet with President Johnson during the Selma crisis. I helped integrate apartments for military personnel. I picketed; I marched; I cried out for peace and human rights. And sometimes I was heard—but not often. Where can a man, one with religious commitment who believes in democracy, work for orderly and rapid change in a reluctant community or institution which finds it easier to maintain the *status quo?*

I was disturbed about Vietnam. I had been disturbed ever since my African experience at the time of Dien Bien Phu. I am not, nor have I ever been, a pacifist, but the more I studied the war in Vietnam, the less I could support the United States position. Little by little, I became convinced that we were wrong about Vietnam and that we should remove all of our forces. Dr. Dana McLean Greeley, who is the immediate past president of the Unitarian Universalist Association, had told me in 1964 that I would come to the conclusion that the Vietnam war was wrong. He was one of the first persons who was a major religious figure to come out wholeheartedly against the war. I also had the opportunity down in Selma to talk to the Reverend Mr. James Bevel, who is one of the leading figures of the Southern Christian Leadership Conference, which Dr. Martin Luther King, Jr. headed at that time. His opinion was the same as Dana Greeley's only more forceful.

By 1966, I was totally convinced that the United States was wrong in its actions in Vietnam, and I was further convinced that the United States was trying to apply *pax Americana* throughout the world with the use of our armed forces. I am sufficiently a student of history to know that *pax Romana* didn't work, and neither did *pax Brittanica*.

7

There are always wars and rumors of wars whenever peace is imposed by external forces through the use of arms.

I arrived in Lexington, Massachusetts, in September of 1968 and became minister of First Parish Church on November 1 of that year. I had always believed and expected that the Constitution of the United States would be adhered to. The Warren Court was one of my great models of what a Supreme Court should be. It was a court that was willing to tackle social issues—even political issues—if the Constitution of the United States was not being followed. I felt that the decision of *Brown* v. *Board of Education of Topeka, Kansas* was a monumental case. This decision ended the concept of "separate but equal," thus ending the legalized separation of public schools in the South. I also thought that *Baker* v. *Carr*—the one-man, one-vote decision—was very significant as we moved toward the concept of participation politics— that one citizen really counted as much as another citizen. And I believed that surely the question of United States involvement in foreign wars would be questioned by someone. As I understood the Constitution, it seemed to me that Congress alone had the right to declare war—not the President. Yet, during the Korean War we had the action under the United Nations. Those of us who were liberal, as we call ourselves, did not question the legality of the war then. But I look back at it now and question its legality. I do not question the fact that those who fought in it were dedicated, nor do I necessarily feel that the United States was wrong in doing what it did; but I feel that the Congress should have been involved.

I reread my United States Constitution. I saw again under Article I, Section 8 that it states clearly that Congress shall have the right to declare war. I am familiar with the debate that went on in Philadelphia during the Constitutional Convention when it was suggested that the President should have the right to declare war. This was resoundingly rejected, for to allow the President to have such unlimited powers all by himself would give him the "kingly" powers that had been the very reason for the Revolution.

I live in an historic house—the house that belonged to Jonathan Harrington. He was one of the Minute Men; he was engaged in the first battle of the Revolution, which took place in his front yard, now the Battle Green in Lexington. He died on April 19, 1775. It does something to one to live in such a house. I never realized that before I moved in. Every morning, I look out the window on the Green where the flag flies day and night in commemoration of the place where the

American Revolution began. What was it all about? It was for the right of people to participate in the decision-making process, in what the government does. And the process of government that most involves people, their lives, their pocketbooks is war.

But time has gone by and the Supreme Court did not rule on this issue. Cases were presented, yet nothing happened. *Certiorari*—the technical word used for the court's granting on its own volition the right to hear on issue—was denied by the court that I had held in such high esteem. I wondered what could be done. Meanwhile, many students in Lexington were coming to see me and question me, even as they had in the Mt. Vernon area of Virginia. "John, what can we do? It is hopeless. None of us count. The government no longer belongs to the people."

I knew that a citizen could petition the Great and General Court to effect legislation for the entire Commonwealth of Massachusetts. I worked during my first year in Lexington to try and introduce a Bill questioning the constitutionality of the war, but was unsuccessful. I was involved in the ABM hearing in Lexington and became interested in technology and new cities and ecology, dreaming futilely of what our priorities should be but were *not* in this great country, because of the war that continued to escalate in Southeast Asia. My Bill began to make even more sense to me. I began to work harder and to dream bigger. Moratorium time came and Governor Sargent, at my invitation, spoke on the Lexington Green on October 15, 1969. He spoke, clearly and unequivocally, for an end to the war in Vietnam.

Congressman Brad Morse supported my efforts on the Bill. Steve Worth, a professor at Northeastern University, was convinced that the war in Vietnam was unconstitutional and offered support and assistance. Kenneth P. O'Donnell, one of President John Kennedy's chief advisors, offered to find me a state representative to introduce the Bill. Larry Adler, a Boston attorney and member of my church, helped me to draft the original Bill, which I introduced under my signature but through a State Representative—Jim Shea—who, Kenny O'Donnell said, could keep an open mind.

At this point in time, December 3, 1969, I had no idea the legislation would pass. The most I hoped to accomplish was to raise again this vital question of who has the power to take us to war. The method was legal, within the system. I believe in the democratic process; I am not a revolutionary. I threw a pebble in the water (to quote Charlie Whipple, chief editorial writer for the *Boston Globe*) and watched the circles spread across the state.

At this juncture Jim Shea took over the leadership. The process now was political, the question constitutional. We met in the crowded cubicle that Massachusetts provides for its legislators. Present with me were Jim Shea; Steve Worth; Dick Cauchi from CPP (Citizens for Participation Politics); John Businger, Jim's new legislative assistant; Mary Ann Seitz, publicity chairman from First Parish Church, Lexington; David Lustig, graduate student from Northeastern; Tom Evans, one of the Harvard Divinity students working at First Parish; and Ron Rosenblith, a young political aspirant from Brookline who knew almost everybody in the State House.

David Lustig is one of the brightest and most dynamic young public relations experts around. He knows the media people and has the audacity to set up press conferences for still untried issues. The meeting ended with a plan for David to set up a press conference for Shea in the State House on January 26, 1970. A freshman State Representative normally does not call a press conference, but then Jim Shea was not an ordinary freshman State Representative. The three persons called upon to speak were Jim, Steve, and myself. The coordination of all activities henceforth was assigned to Mary Ann Seitz. David Lustig would handle PR, Dick Cauchi agreed to keep all 131 CPP groups alerted. John Businger was to aid Jim at the State House, thus keeping Jim as free as possible to lobby there for the Bill. Ron Rosenblith would begin the process of seeking support from political figures with whom he had close personal connections. I was given the task of financing the venture. At this time our bank roll was one hundred dollars.

The meeting broke up, but Steve, Jim, and I had immediate work to accomplish. Jim had called and asked if the Bill could be discharged from Public Safety and assigned to the Judiciary Committee. This was agreed to and a hearing was scheduled for February 11, 1970. Our press conference on January 26 would be the opening door to spread the word to all the State that the issue was real, was serious, and was the issue behind which all peace activities should coordinate. Yet so much more was needed.

Steve Worth was superb. He agreed to dictate a brief, not in legal style but more in logical style. I agreed to write to all lawyers in the area who had previously worked for peace activities. I further agreed to seek out the necessary volunteers to do all the mimeographing, folding, assembling, and mailing that would be forthcoming. The tasks were far greater than we at first could have imagined.

The press conference came off beautifully. We were carried on local TV stations and received good press coverage in most local papers. We were not yet national in scope, but at that stage it was in the General Court of Massachusetts that the fate of H.B. 2396 lay.

Stillman Williams, a good friend in Lexington, had arranged a dinner party at his home on January 26 for me to become better acquainted with his cousin Charles Whipple, editor of the editorial page of the *Boston Globe*. By this time Steve Worth had prepared a one-page rationale supporting the argument for the Bill. I had copies of H.B. 2396 plus copies of various letters, speeches, and statements that Jim Shea, Steve Worth, and I had prepared. Coincidentally, the dinner party was interrupted by Jim Westover of WEEI, local CBS station for Boston, who had some questions to ask me. This whetted Charlie Whipple's interest in H.B. 2396, and the first editorial dealing with the Bill appeared in the *Boston Globe* the next Friday. We were on our way.

A busy way it was. Steve, Jim, and I made our time available for public appearances, debates, or media. We appeared on TV, on talk shows, and at church and civic gatherings. WEEI, particularly Gene Burns, was interested in the Bill and gave it great exposure. Steve somehow managed to dictate the brief. I asked Liz Williams to type, mimeograph, and collate six hundred copies. The demands from lawyers for supporting arguments were now met and some money did come in. Time still was too pressing.

Jim Shea managed the legislative procedures. The two people most important to the next hurdle were Senator Joseph Ward of Fitchburg and Representative Cornelius Kiernan from Lowell. Massachusetts is one of the few states in the Union that has joint House-Senate committees. The Judiciary Committee is made up entirely of lawyers, is a well-respected committee, and has an unusually high percentage of favorably reported bills enacted by the General Court. We needed not only to convince the Judiciary Committee that this was a just and legal matter; but we needed also to convince them it was politically possible at this moment in time.

Steve Worth set about to find the best legal talents in the country to appear at the hearing. Lawrence Velvel, Professor of Constitutional Law at the University of Kansas, had recently published an exhaustive article in the *Kansas Law Review* dealing with the unsettled constitutional question of presidential war powers and congressional war powers. He agreed to appear. Michael Tigar, Professor of Constitutional Law at

11

U.C.L.A. and one of the most active young lawyers in the peace movement on the West Coast, also consented to come. Professor Warren Schwartz of the University of Illinois joined our parade of experts. It was my task to find national figures to join our effort. A close friend of mine in Washington is a close friend of former Senator Ernest Gruening of Alaska. Senator Gruening agreed to appear. Jim Shea worked closely with the Judiciary Committee to set up an orderly and dignified hearing.

Mr. Fred King from Newton, Massachusetts, has been called the "Johnny Appleseed" of the Bill. He had been active in political organization in Newton. He was active in the peace world and was closely associated with CPP. He took over the printing and distribution of hand bills and mail outs. We immediately printed eighty thousand leaflets with the wording of the Bill on one side and information for political action on the other. The costs were suspended, by using personal credit, and five- and ten-dollar contributions began to come in.

CPP turned on its telephone trees. The Lexington youth, already tuned in by their presence at the press conference, met and urged other high school groups to join the effort. Jack Powers from the Beacon Hill Support Group volunteered to aid in directing and monitoring the expected crowds at the State House on February 11.

The hearing was impressive. Senator Gruening told me he had never seen a legislative hearing more dignified and persuasive. Senator Ward was a strong but open-minded chairman. Some twelve hundred people came, a good mixture of young and older people. The hearing was held at the Gardner Auditorium. All the 800 seats were filled, people stood in the lobby, and others were turned away for lack of room. The atmosphere was courteous and respectful. No untoward incident marred the occasion. Witness after witness appeared before the microphone. Jim managed their sequence with just the right touch. Legal experts and a former United States Senator led the way and were followed by Gold Star Mothers and wounded veterans from Vietnam. Ministers, college professors, housewives, all came forward to support our Bill. It was the result of a momentous effort on our part, but it was so much more. It was an outpouring of the desire of people to make the representative system work.

And it did work. We realized at the outset that there were many problems with the original draft of the Bill. We sought help and were given it. Senator Beryl Cohen suggested we see Mr. William Homans, a respected attorney in Boston, known for his participation in the Spock trials. Bill made suggestions. We listened carefully to Larry Velvel. We worked continually and closely with Mr. Robert Condlin, a young attorney in the Attorney General's office. Larry Adler met with us again and again. We made drafts and redrafts. We offered our suggestions to the Judiciary Committee. They worked themselves in long sessions trying to perfect the Bill for which there is no legislative precedent.

During the period between February 11, 1970 and the first weeks in March when the Judiciary Committee was to report out the Bill, Jim, Steve, and I were again on the circuit of talks, radio appearances, and meetings with groups large and small. The continued outpouring of support came from sources all over the state.

Dr. Robin Remington, a lovely young Ph.D. teaching at M.I.T., was one of our mainstays. She organized petitions, stood in theatre lines gathering signatures, spoke to numerous groups. She was really turned on to the system and knew how to project her feelings. She was joined by school teachers in Saugus, and housewives in Fitchburg. The mail to State Senators and State Representatives poured in at a rate of more than ten to one in support of the Bill.

The Judiciary Committee listened to the carefully prepared arguments. It worked long hours composing the final draft to present to the House of Representatives. It listened as well to the people of the Commonwealth of Massachusetts. The issue was joined. The debates in the House began.

According to those present, H.B. 2396 was the most thoroughly debated and carefully heard citizen's petition ever to go through the Massachusetts legislature. There was serious opposition. Representative Hogan, representing the veterans' organizations and his own carefully prepared view, led the fight arguing that the Bill gave comfort to the enemy, was nothing more than states' rights, and should be referred to the next annual session, a maneuver intended to defeat the measure. The floor fight for the Bill was led by Representative Kiernan, House Chairman of the Judiciary Committee.

The Speaker, the Hon. David Bartley, was convinced both by the logic of the merits of the Bill and by the logic of political support that the measure should pass. There were many speculations that the Democratic majority was seeking to embarrass the Republican governor. There was talk of the need for the Speaker to regain favor with liberals, because the reduction in size of the House was not sent for referendum.

In the game of politics many events play their parts, but there was no doubt about the main issue. Could the Commonwealth of Massachusetts play a vital part in determining and protecting the federal constitutional rights of its citizens? The legal arguments are not conclusive. The Supreme Court in 1945 had permitted the State of Georgia to seek and protect the economic rights of Georgia citizens. Later, in 1957, the Supreme Court held that a treaty was not a higher obligation than the United States Constitution. The President, it is true, has down through our history dispatched American military forces to foreign engagements without consent of the Congress. The issue was joined on the floor of the House.

The issue, debated for hours and hours, was the very issue that had bothered me in Morocco, that had bothered me in Selma, that had bothered me in my churches in Alexandria and in Lexington. Do we live under a government where our rights as citizens are protected and guaranteed by the United States Constitution, or have we given to the President alone or to anyone else, the right, the final authority, to determine what those rights and best interests might be?

The vote to postpone the Bill until the next annual session was finally called. A vote "no" meant the Bill would stay alive. In the House the vote is electronic. Red is no, green is yes, as simple as that. As I watched, at last there were 116 red, 110 green. We had passed another major battle. We had won.

Jim Shea was a quiet man in many ways but a terribly self-contained man. He had a hard time really relaxing. That night we ate together at the Parker House Hotel. There was no time to celebrate—it was Thursday night; the next vote would be Monday. The call for a turnout of all support against the Bill had been made by the veterans' organizations and other groups. We held a strategy meeting as we celebrated our first vote victory in the House. We selected those state representatives who might possibly switch. We urged supportive calls to those who were with us and pressure calls to those who were against us. Mrs. John Webb, secretary to Massachusetts PAX, the leader of the peace groups in the state, offered much help, guidance, and assistance. Robin Remington, Sharon Schofield, and Elizabeth Latzer worked all weekend. Lee Goldstein from Saugus turned-on her high-schoolers. A Lexington group sought to pressure Lincoln Cole, our representative, to join us. CPP cranked up the telephone trees again. A massive effort was made by Jack Powers and the Beacon Hill Support Group. Jim called for all the power the Speaker could muster. State senators in favor were asked to call their district representatives. The press was most helpful.

Steve Worth organized a telephone effort to obtain support from other nationally known constitutional lawyers. Some of the most respected constitutional law professors from across the country responded. These included:

Quincy Wright, University of Virginia
Wallace McClure, University of Virginia
Hans J. Morgenthau, University of Chicago
Richard Falk, Princeton University
John Flackett, Peter Donovan, David Carroll, and Sherman Katz, all of Boston College
Vernon Countryman, Harvard Law School
Edward Sparer, University of Pennsylvania Law School
Clyde Summers, Yale Law School
Lawrence Velvel, University of Kansas Law School
William C. Rice and Gordon Cunningham, University of Wisconsin Law School
Warren Schwartz, University of Illinois Law School
Richard E. Webb and Richard S. Miller, Ohio State Law School
John Fried and John Herz, City College of New York
Burns Weston, University of Iowa Law School
Alan Dershowitz, Harvard Law School
William P. Homans, Jr., Boston lawyer and former Member of the House

The *Boston Globe* gave much space to our efforts. Bob Turner, Ken Campbell, David Nyhan, and others were in constant contact to cover our efforts. WEEI again followed with great interest all that was happening and kept their talk shows open for comments. Mr. Richard Gaines of UPI kept the national wires hot with breaking events.

The vote on Monday followed more hours of debate. The turn-on had paid off, not for the veterans' organizations but for the peace movement. We won by an even longer majority, 136 to 89. We knew we would win in the Senate. I was confident the governor would sign the Bill.

It had been an exhausting but exhilarating battle—the first time that any legislation at any level of government dealing directly with the Vietnam war had been put to the political test and had won.

The governor did sign the Bill. April 2 was a warm, bright day in Boston. There was an overflow crowd in the governor's office. The television, radio, and press people with all their equipment seemed almost casual now. The governor signed the Bill. He looked up at me as the last camera flashed. I asked him for the pen. He smiled that quizzical smile that Governor Sargent smiles and handed me the blue felt pen. We shook hands.

But now I think of Jim Shea. My joy in knowing him has not been diminished by his death. He had that peculiar spark of leadership that should not have been taken from us. He was fearless and yet totally humble. Jim Shea is dead, but his ideas and ideals will live on. I am glad the Bill is called the Shea Bill. I stood for a moment with Sen. Edward Kennedy at Jim's funeral. He, like all the rest of us, wondered why. So many people have asked me that. I knew Jim. I knew him well. We had long times together to talk, to explore, to wonder. Where are we going? Where is our country going?

Jim Shea gave his life to public service. He was too much alone. He never learned to be angry. He never vented his anger. He was quiet. He was humble. He was tired.

I do not know why Jim took his life. I only know he was tired. Jim and I talked of a new America—a new America where there would be room for all in all our differences. We spoke of legislation to build new cities, to provide better Medicare, to aid the young, to comfort the elderly. We spoke of legislation to tie cuts in the defense budget to additions to those items we felt made up QHL, the Quality of Human Life.

Jim spent the last few months of his life continually working for peace through the system, trying to realize the American dream of justice, equality, brotherhood, peace, and love. Jim Shea is dead, but the Shea Bill is already living history.

Senator J. William Fulbright told me that the action of the Commonwealth of Massachusetts awakened the conscience of the Congress. The Hatfield-McGovern resolution brings to the national legislature the exact issue that we seek to have tested in the Supreme Court. Our experience has proved that the system can work if *we* will work within it. I accept that legacy passed to me from Jim and others like him. I share it with all I meet and know. The American dream of the worth and dignity and value of every citizen can be protected and realized only if each of us is committed to make it work.

3   Old Politics for a New Cause

Kenneth D. Campbell

Jim Shea's Bill challenging presidential wars was given little chance of passage when it was first introduced into the Massachusetts Legislature. But it succeeded. It succeeded because it was an idea whose time had come, and because it had both "new politicians" and "old politicians" working for it, albeit for different reasons. In my opinion it probably never would have passed except for some unrelated, strictly political matters. The Democratic Legislature had been embarrassed by the public beating it had taken from Republican Gov. Francis W. Sargent, the press, and the public for the Legislature's adamant stand against a reform that would have eliminated the jobs of 80 of the 240 state representataives. The legislative leadership, Senate Pres. Maurice A. Donahue, 52, and his legislative protégé and fellow townsman from Holyoke, Speaker David M. Bartley, 35, were eager to embarrass Sargent in return.

Moreover, Donahue was a candidate for the Democratic nomination for governor in the state that had rejected Richard M. Nixon by a margin of 696,000 votes in 1968. Clearly, the politically smart move would be to tie Frank Sargent, a handsome, liberal Republican with a good public image, to the unpopular coattails of President Nixon and make Nixon's unpopular policies a major campaign issue in the 1970 election in Massachusetts. Sargent, however, outmaneuvered them. What Donahue did not count on was that Nixon agreed with Sargent that the governor might have to sign the Bill in order to survive the Fall election.

As an attempt to embarrass Sargent and Nixon, the Donahue-Bartley tactics on the Shea Bill were spectacularly unsuccessful. After much indecision and hesitation, Sargent signed the Bill and stole the headlines and television interviews. Donahue and Bartley were proud of the Vietnam Bill as a legislative achievement; as a matter of political gain they had to be chagrined. Robert Yasi, Sargent's chief secretary, summed up the political gains of the Bill when he privately kidded Jim Shea, "It was the Shea Bill, but it is the Sargent law."

A Petition to Congress

Donahue had not always supported the entire Bill. At the February 11 hearing, he expressed his doubt that the Legislature would approve the use of the Massachusetts attorney general to force a Supreme Court decision. He did express, however, what he termed his "complete support" for the Bill's policy statement that a citizen should not have to fight an undeclared war.

Without the support of Donahue, the Senate president for six years and a man who commands tremendous respect from his fellow legislators and the press, the Legislature probably would not have approved the Bill. At the hearing, Donahue recommended different machinery to accomplish a similar policy. He recommended that the Legislature pass a resolution asking Congress to begin action on a constitutional amendment that would bar the President from using draftees in undeclared wars.

But Donahue was almost alone at the hearing in his stand. The only other witness to express doubts about the Bill was a "Bible Funda-mentalist" who said the Army had been denied victory in Vietnam because of the lack of adequate leaders and arms.

The main witnesses for the Bill were legal experts from all over the country who had been marshalled to the Massachusetts Legislature by the authors of the Bill, the Reverend John M. Wells and Prof. Steve Worth, and by its sponsor, Rep. H. James Shea, Jr.

The experts impressed the committee and the eight-hundred-odd spectators who overflowed an auditorium in the basement of the Massachusetts State House.

"It was overwhelming," said House Judiciary Chairman Cornelius F. Kiernan, a distinguished-looking white-haired Democrat from Lowell who is known as "the Silver Fox." Kiernan is not known for being particularly liberal, so his comment on the Bill is interesting. "I am sure," he said, "that the vast majority of the members were completely convinced that there is not one scintilla of legal justification for being in Vietnam."

The Senate Chairman of the joint committee, Sen. Joseph D. Ward of Fitchburg, said, "I've been here twenty years and I've never seen a group like them. I was persuaded that a confrontation between the state and federal governments would be a healthy thing." Ward has a reputation as a liberal Democrat. He said, "When I first read the Bill, I was inclined to be opposed. It appeared patently unconstitutional."

After the hearing, Ward had changed his view but he still doubted that the Bill was in proper constitutional form. Kiernan feared the Bill might be a "cruel hoax" by failing to get a favorable ruling from the United States Supreme Court. Other legislators and assistants to Atty. Gen. Robert H. Quinn also expressed doubts about the Bill's constitutionality.

The Wells Bill

At this point, the Bill was as John Wells had submitted it to Shea on December 3, 1969, the deadline for the filing of 1970 legislation. Wells had been searching for a sponsor for the Bill for a year and found Shea through Kenneth P. O'Donnell, the former chief aide to President Kennedy. Wells turned to O'Donnell for help because he knew of O'Donnell's long-standing opposition to the Vietnam war. O'Donnell was the only politician of national renown who supported the Bill. Massachusetts Sens. Edward M. Kennedy and Edward W. Brooke, although known for their disputes with the Nixon administration over the conduct of the war, never entered into the controversy over the Vietnam Bill.

Shea agreed to submit the legislation "by request." Legislation "by request," or the right of free petition, is a peculiarity of the Massachusetts legislative process that helped produce 6108 Bills for the consideration of the 1970 legislature by the December 3, 1969 filing deadline. The right of "free petition" gives Massachusetts citizens the right to draft their own legislation when they think "there ought to be a law." Free petition consequently results in hundreds of crank Bills, which become a big headache to the House and Senate counsel who have to rewrite the Bills to put them into proper legislative form.

Ideally, free petition is an expression of democracy in action and every once in a while, as in the case of the Vietnam Bill, a citizen turns up with a good idea which becomes law.

Legislation filed "by request" usually means that the representative or senator is taking no position on the legislation, but merely filing it as a favor to his constituent. That was the case with Wells's Bill on undeclared wars.

Jim Shea

Shea, 30, a political science graduate of Tufts University who had done graduate study at the University of Virginia Law School and Tufts, was extremely busy in December. He was in the second session of his first term in the House and had filed about fifty Bills, including major proposals on divorce reform, election law reform, and on a youth environment corps. Sympathetic to the anti-war cause, he said he filed the Bill before he had time to read it. After studying it, he enthusiastically endorsed it.

The Bill took up most of the rest of Shea's short life. Shea was a somewhat shy man. He wore thick, dark-rimmed glasses. Soft-spoken, he had an incisive mind. His wry smile began at the left side of his mouth and never quite wrinkled the right side of his thin lips. "He smiled warily, as though afraid the smile would not be returned," wrote Peter Lucas of the Boston *Herald Traveler* when Shea, troubled by the pressure of intense work, committed suicide on May 9. It was five weeks after the freshman legislator won passage of the Vietnam Bill through a hostile House.

Through the Mill

On January 26, 1970 Shea, Wells, and Prof. Steve Worth of Northeastern University held a press conference at the State House to try to evoke public support for the Bill, House Bill No. 2396.

The Bill had a broad scope. It allowed a citizen of Massachusetts to notify the attorney general of Massachusetts if the citizen "serving in the military forces" was ordered to "a combat zone or other area where actual hostilities have been in existence for more than sixty days from the time of commencement of said hostilities," provided that Congress had not declared war there. The attorney general, in turn, was required to "take the necessary and appropriate actions" to implement the right of the citizen not to have to serve in an undeclared war "outside the continental limits of the United States." It further defined a combat zone as "any area in which casualties or deaths from military or naval action have taken place within sixty days after the initial deployment of the United States armed forces in such area."

In other words, no Massachusetts man—draftee or volunteer—could be sent to Vietnam against his wishes without the Defense Department's incurring a suit. The much-used "emergency powers" of the Commander-in-Chief would be limited to such an extent that for instance, President Eisenhower's use of troops in Lebanon for five months in 1958 would have been barred.

Reverend Wells pointed out during the January press conference: "Now we have forty-six thousand troops in Thailand, more than double the number that were in Vietnam in 1964. Do we commit *these* troops and our nation to war? Do we do so by the action of a President alone? Such a course is both unconstitutional and immoral. As a religious person I protest. As a lawyer I seek a legal remedy." Wells said the constitutional rights of Massachusetts citizens "are denied if the President has assumed the right to declare war, a power clearly given to the Congress and only to Congress. . . . Right now, over twelve thousand Massachusetts citizens are required to serve in combat zones without proper constitutional authorization."

Wells was familiar with the Pentagon. He had served there from 1957 to 1969 as a legislative liaison between the Defense Department and state governments. A Unitarian minister in Lexington, he spoke well. Northern liberals conditioned to distrust Southerners hardly could believe that such thoughts were spoken in the thin, syrupy tones of Wells's native Georgia. A short man, slightly balding with grey-brown sideburns which extend an inch below his ears, Wells—like a good politician—was always ready with a firm handshake or an arm around the back of a newsman or legislator.

Worth, the Northeastern University professor of political science, talked rapidly at the conference, unlike Wells. Tall, with a wrinkled forehead, his hair was brushed forward in the style of the Romans of two thousand years ago. At the outset of his statement during the press conference, he sought to dispel the notion that the Bill was a Massachusetts counterpart to the Southern Doctrine of interposition. "That device," he said,

> employed by a number of the Southern states, sought to interpose the power of the "sovereign state" between a federal court order issued under

the *final* [his emphasis] constitutional authority of the United States and the affected citizen of that state. It was the use of state legislative power attempting to evade (or more realistically, delay) the promulgation of an established constitutional rule. The confrontation manifest in interposition was between state legislative power and well-established constitutional authority.

Worth said, "Our argument is that the courts have not yet ruled squarely on the constitutional validity of the President's assumption of the power to declare war. Indeed, that is what we seek here to establish. The confrontation envisaged in our legislation is between state legislative power and what we claim is an unconstitutional usurpation of federal executory power."

Worth concluded, "We seek a constitutional rule. We do not seek to avoid it once that rule is established." In essence, the Bill did not constitute interposition because interposition had placed the state between its citizens and a court-interpreted federal law. The Wells-Shea legislation was not interposition, because there was no firm law on the constitutionality of an undeclared war.

Worth also noted that the Bill:

does not challenge peace-time conscription authorized by Congress. It does not contest the proper role of executory power in deploying American troops consistent with treaty obligations authorized by Congress pursuant to the United Nations charter. What it does say in this respect is that the Congress must affirm any presidential military action by a formal declaration of war under such an activation of treaty obligations within a sixty-day period as a necessary precondition to the use of any except volunteer troops.

Since the Bill referred to Massachusetts citizens both "inducted or serving in the military forces," it is difficult to see how Worth justified his contention that the President could use volunteer troops beyond the sixty-day period without seeking a declaration of war.

Shea emphasized at the press conference that:

The Constitution under Article I, Section 8 places a specific power to declare war in the Congress. It is our theory that this power to declare war cannot be constitutionally delegated to the President. Consequently, the vague Gulf of Tonkin Resolution constitutes no such declaration of war. Nor can it be construed to be a delegation of that congressional responsibility. The only presidential power in this area of initiating war is implied in Article II, Section 2—the implied emergency powers stemming from the constitutional designation of the President as the Commander-in-Chief of the military. We fully recognize the supremacy of power properly exercised under the federal Constitution in accord with Article VI.

Our contention, however, is that the Vietnam war is illegal and unconstitutional under the President's emergency powers in the absence of a Congressional declaration of war. The very telling fact that the United

States has been at a factual level of war for a longer period than it took us to win the double-theatered World War II, and the fact that Congress has been readily available during these five years of sustained hostilities clearly indicates that any presidential authority to wage this war under the implied emergency powers was long ago exhausted. This bill is aimed at protecting the people of Massachusetts from an unconstitutional exercise of federal power.

This brought applause from forty Lexington High School students who attended the press conference "as an educational project." Their attendance was the first public indication of the strong support the Bill was to draw from young people, who crowded the House and Senate galleries every time the Bill was debated.

Shea already had accomplished his first legislative feat for the Bill. The clerk of the House had mistakenly assigned the Bill to the Public Safety Committee, chaired by Rep. Ralph Sirianni of Winthrop. Shea knew Sirianni would prove to be one of the adamant foes of the Bill, and the Bill never would have emerged from Sirianni's committee. Shea therefore quickly contacted Speaker Bartley to transfer the Bill to the more sympathetic Judiciary Committee, which scheduled a public hearing for Ash Wednesday, February 11.

The Hearing

The hearing was a tremendous success. Unlike Congressional committees, legislative committees in Massachusetts are not accustomed to hearing distinguished academicians and expert lawyers discuss legislation. Shea directed the three-hour presentation, bringing on Prof. Lawrence Velvel from the University of Kansas, Prof. Michael Tigar from the University of California at Los Angeles, Prof. Warren Schwartz from the University of Illinois, and former Sen. Ernest Gruening from Alaska.

Wells told the committee he drafted the Bill as he looked across historic Lexington Common and pondered the thought that the United States had reverted to "the same tyrannical situation" that had existed in colonial times. The power of the United States President, he said, is now "the same that the king of England had."

Velvel testified that the Bill could settle "the most profound, the most far-reaching constitutional issue of our times." He noted that he had tried to get the Supreme Court to rule on the issue of presidential power in a recent case, *Velvel* v. *Nixon*, but that the court had declined to rule in his case and dozens of other individual cases. He said there were indications that the court would take into consideration a case where there was a substantial interest, such as the support of a state Legislature.

Worth emphasized that the Bill was important to youth, because it would show them that "the system" still worked.

Tigar noted that the debates of the 1787 Constitutional Convention clearly showed that the drafters of the Constitution—when they changed the wording to give Congress the power to "declare" war rather than "wage" war—intended to give the President the power only to repel sudden attacks, not to wage foreign wars.

Schwartz urged the committee to approve the Bill. He said the matter should be decided in court. "The Bill deals with enormously difficult questions which have no business being decided at demonstrations." Gruening, one of the first senators to oppose the war strongly, said Congress had been deceived by false information in August, 1964, when it passed the Gulf of Tonkin Resolution. "The Vietnam war," said Gruening, "is the greatest folly that we have committed in our history."

Representatives of students groups and peace organizations said the Bill offered hope of success within the system.

The strongest criticism of the Bill at the February 11 hearing was offered by Donahue. The Senate president, while saying that he was "prepared to support the Bill," went on to say that he condemned the Bill's legal machinery as ineffective and inappropriate. He said he believed that he knew of a more responsible method of winning the same objectives. In essence, Donahue liked the policy of the Bill, not the machinery it used to implement that policy.

Donahue is tall, with a slight paunch, receding and greying hair, and glasses. His voice is low; his manner is gruff, abrupt, and to the point. He enumerated his objections to House Bill 2396.

He began by giving his "complete support" to "the general statement of public policy." He said that on Vietnam Moratorium Day (October 15, 1969) he had addressed the student body at Bridgewater State College and urged essentially the same proposition:

> I said at that time that no American should be drafted into the Armed Services and sent to fight outside the continental limits of the United States without a declaration of war by the Congress of the United States. I called for the adoption of an amendment to the United States Constitution that would spell out clearly and unmistakably the rights of American young men conscripted for military service not to be required to fight overseas unless and until the Congress of the United States authorized such action by a clear and unequivocal formal declaration of war.

Donahue proposed "the creation of a volunteer professional army." He said:

The well-paid, well-trained volunteer professional fighting force would be instantly available to the President to fight police actions or put out brushfire wars, to react immediately to breaches of America's treaty obligations and commitments. But no young man who was conscripted into military service could be compelled to fight overseas purely by executive order.

Having listed his differences, the Senate president said, "Whether the narrower proposition which I have earlier espoused, or the broader proposition as embodied in House No. 2396 which I am today prepared to support, is the preferable formulation is a matter for individual judgment—and for the collective judgment of your committee."

Donahue noted that his proposal gave draftees even more protection than House 2396. "My earlier proposal would absolutely prohibit draftees from fighting overseas without a declaration of war by the United States Congress; the proposition contained in the Bill before you would permit draftees to fight overseas for up to sixty days before requiring a Congressional declaration of war."

Donahue went on to condemn as neither "effective, workable nor appropriate" the method of implementing House 2396—the citizen's serving notice to the state attorney general:

I am particularly troubled that this implementing method—this attempt to seek through state action, as Professor Worth of Northeastern University has put it, "to force a Constitutional resolution of a profound and unsettled Constitutional issue," may well create unnecessary and unneeded hostility to the essential proposition.

I believe that there is a more affirmative, more constructive and more responsible method of achieving the objectives of those who in good faith, and from sincere conviction, are supporting this legislation. I believe that the general statement of public policy, narrow or broad, should be embodied in a resolution memorializing the Congress of the United States to initiate appropriate action to amend the United States Constitution along the lines of the general statement. Unless this is done, I am fearful that the entire Bill will not be passed by the General Court (the Massachusetts Legislature) and the general statement of public policy, which I believe many members of the legislature would and could support, will also be defeated. . . . The complex question of whether or not the Vietnam war is illegal or unconstitutional is not, I respectfully submit, a question which can or should be resolved by action of the Massachusetts state legislature.

Donahue added, "Massachusetts can still lead the nation by becoming the first state to request officially that a constitutional amendment be adopted clarifying the limits of presidential power to order citizens serving in the Armed Forces overseas."

The problem with the cautious proposal of Donahue was that it takes years to pass a Constitutional amendment through Congress. Further, it was doubtful that as many as thirty-eight of the fifty states would back such a proposal, as required for a Constitutional amendment.

Shea realized however, that Donahue had made some potent points with the committee. Shea quickly went to work to mend the holes in the Bill. The hearing was on a Wednesday. Over the weekend, Shea worked with Wells, Worth, attorney Larry Adler of Lexington and aides to Attorney General Quinn. On Tuesday, February 17, Shea presented Senator Ward with a new draft of the Bill. Ward, after viewing the new draft, said the committee would review the various proposals to see, "if there isn't some method by which we can make this a viable vehicle."

The House Cut

The Vietnam Bill all this time was playing understudy on the public stage to the controversy raging over the proposal to cut the size of the House by one third.

The House cut proposal was initiated two years earlier by the League of Women Voters. Their argument was that a House of Representatives composed of 160 members, rather than 240 members, would make the legislative process more efficient. The $912,000 saved by eliminating the $11,400 annual salaries of 80 representatives could be used to hire legislative assistants and secretaries for the understaffed legislators, many of whom do not even have desks.

But there also were some powerful reform arguments opposed to the House cut. Spokesmen for black and Puerto Rican minority groups said the House cut would cut down their chances for representation in the House. Of the 240 representatives, two from Boston were black, a ratio of 1/120. The black population of Massachusetts has a ratio of about 1/45 to the white population.

There were partisan arguments. Young liberals feared that the seats that would be lost would be from their ranks if they were forced to run against old-guard representatives who used the job as a political power base. Republican representatives feared that the cuts would simply mean that their few seats would further decline. Democratic Party loyalists, used to having their way on redistricting because the predominantly Democratic county commissioners draw the lines, were worried that a special redistricting commission would hurt them.

The House cut issue was scheduled to go on the November, 1970 ballot if it could win the approval of at least one quarter of the legislators. But the Democrats have a two-thirds majority in both branches of the Legislature, enough to override the governor's vote. Sargent favored the cut, as did an overwhelming majority of Massachusetts citizens, according to a *Boston Globe* poll. But Sargent, the people, and the League of Women Voters lost.

Although the Democrats had won their legislative battle, the image of the Legislature was at rock bottom. To vindicate themselves in the eyes of the voters, Democratic leaders Bartley and Donahue decided to go all-out for the Shea Bill, since the peace issue was even more popular than representational reform. In the bargain they still hoped to embarrass Sargent politically, by putting him in the position of voting against his Republican President on the issue of the Vietnam war.

A Political Deal?

When Bartley announced March 11 that he would support the Shea Bill and speak for it, newsmen noted that Shea was one of the few young liberal Democrats who had backed Bartley on the House cut issue. They noted, with political approval, that Bartley called it "the Shea Bill" and assumed that the Speaker was giving the Newton legislator the credit in gratitude for his vote against the House cut. Newsmen who had favored both the House cut and the Vietnam Bill agreed privately that if the House cut vote was the price Jim Shea had to pay to get the Vietnam Bill to the floor with the Speaker's support, then it was worth it. In Vietnam, after all, men's lives were in jeopardy. Only political livelihoods were in jeopardy in the House cut issue. But cynics aren't always right in politics, and the Shea-Bartley combination apparently was a marriage of mutual convenience rather than a shotgun affair arranged by Bartley. Shea, it turned out, had decided to vote against the House cut the previous Fall.

The story didn't come out until after Shea's death. It was told by a shaken John Businger, Shea's twenty-five-year-old administrative and legislative assistant, at a wake-like meeting of Shea's friends at John Wells's house on Lexington Common on the day of Shea's death. To relieve the feeling of depression, the talk was of politics, of funny incidents, of reasons why legislators switched their votes. Someone mentioned that he didn't blame Jim for trading his vote on the House cut for the Vietnam Bill because he thought the Bill was the more important piece of legislation.

27

"That's what everyone thinks," said Businger. "But I know it wasn't true, because I know the date he decided to vote against the House cut, and it was long before he even heard of the Bill.

"It was in June, I think it was June 8, because I left for Navy duty shortly thereafter, and we just began to talk about it in the State House corridor. He was for it, and I was against it. And really, we were just sort of testing out our ideas on one another. When I came back from the Navy in September, I saw Jim across the street on the second day I was back. We chatted, and he said, 'You know, I think I've changed my mind on the House cut since I talked with you.' He knew then, in September, that he was going to vote against it. He didn't even hear about the Vietnam Bill until John Wells brought it to him on December 3.

"Once he decided," said Businger with a smile, "I'm not saying he might not have realized that his vote might stand him in good stead with Speaker Bartley at some future time."

Businger's argument was that reducing representation was not the thing to do in an era of participation politics, and that the eighty losers would include a higher proportion of young liberals than of conservatives who hold positions of power in the legislature. Shea's own seat was not considered to be endangered, because Newton's population had increased and the assumption was that most of the new residents were more liberal than conservative.

To the Floor

Although the House cut vote and the Vietnam Bill weren't linked in Shea's mind, they were in Bartley's. The Speaker took the floor of the House March 12, 1970 for the second time in the two-month-old legislative session and spoke for the Vietnam Bill.

"Two weeks ago," he told the attentive House,

I came to this microphone to urge your rejection of a proposed amendment to the Massachusetts constitution which would have reduced the size of the House of Representatives. I come to this microphone today to urge your support of the so-called Shea Bill on Vietnam, a measure designed to test the constitutionality of the war in Vietnam. I shall not belabor the point, but there are some distinct parallels between my position on these two very different legislative matters. Chief among these is my feeling that it is time for the legislative branch of government to reassert itself—to challenge a trend that has come about perhaps by legislative default in which the chief executive has claimed unto himself legislative powers and prerogatives.

For more than a decade now, those championing reform have canonized creative executive power and lauded its extension on local, state and national levels. But each increase in executive power has resulted in a corresponding loss of legislative power. There is no more glaring example of this on the federal level than the waging of the undeclared war in Vietnam. It makes no sense at this point to seek to determine political culpability for the present situation in Vietnam. It does make eminently good sense though, as Representative Shea contends, for someone or some *body* [Bartley's emphasis] to determine whether or not Congress has abdicated—or has had seized from it—its sole and exclusive Constitutional power to declare war. Congress may be unwilling to make a fight for its own rights. But this legislature—which has seldom backed off from a good scrap—has before it today precedent-setting legislation which could force a determination at the highest level of the constitutionality of the Vietnam war.

If such adjudication finds that the executive has unconstitutionally usurped Congress's war-making powers, then morally and constitutionally those war efforts should be halted pending a declaration of war. And I would doubt that such a declaration would be forthcoming from the people's representatives in Congress.

Why should Massachusetts get involved in a national issue, some will ask. "Why not?" I answer. The beginning of the end of another "limited war"—the infamous Mexican-American war—had its start here. And last October, some one hundred thousand of our citizens gathered on Boston Common publicly to plead for peace. One month ago, eight hundred people jammed Gardner Auditorium in support of this legislation.

But tradition aside, the best reason to get involved is the fact that more than forty thousand young Americans already have died in a war of dubious constitutionality—and the count is still on and climbing. If we pass this legislation today, if the Shea Bill eventually becomes law, then we will have done something important not only for our own people, but for all the people of this nation. For we will have picked up the responsibility abandoned by Congress to advise and not merely consent to an executive who upon occasion, *can be wrong*. [Bartley's emphasis]

"And," the Speaker concluded, "we will have taken a small step toward restoring the legislative branch of government to the role intended it by the framers of our constitution."

It was a good speech to start a 3½ hour debate on the Bill, which had been rewritten considerably in the Judiciary Committee. The Bill, renumbered as House 5165, read in part as follows:

Section 1. No inhabitant of the Commonwealth inducted or serving in the military forces of the United States shall be required to serve outside the territorial limits of the United States in the conduct of armed hostilities not an emergency and not otherwise authorized in the powers granted to the President of the United States in Article II, Section 2 of the Constitution of the United States designating the President as the Commander-in-Chief, unless such hostilities were initially authorized or subsequently ratified by a Congressional declaration of war according to the constitutionally established procedures in Article I, Section 8 of the Constitution of the United States.

Shea, in his address to the House, said,

> What Section 1 does is to identify proper, existing constitutional rights to Congressional participation in the most awesome power a sovereign state can exercise—that decision whether to, or whether not to, commit the lives and resources of its people to war.
> Section 2 mandates to the Attorney General the responsibility of asserting and defending in the name of the Commonwealth this Massachusetts serviceman's constitutional right to have Congress participate in the judgment whether to make war.

"This is the only way, by having the state as an actual party, that Supreme Court review of this constitutional question can be maximized," said Shea. Shea "confessed" to the House that he had not been sure about the Bill when he filed it by request. After studying it, however, he became convinced of its merit. He emphasized that the Bill transcended the Vietnam peace movement in an attempt to settle a grave constitutional question. He noted also that in 1965 he had supported President Johnson in Vietnam and had volunteered for the Army, but was turned away (because of an ulcer).

Judiciary Committee Chairman Cornelius F. Kiernan said the committee had backed the Bill because it was the only avenue of redress for an aggrieved citizen, regardless of one's view on the war.

The opposition was led by a twenty-four-year veteran of the House who was not a lawyer. Gerald P. Lombard is among the 55 representatives in the 240-member House who have not gone beyond high school. Lombard was born and raised in Fitchburg, a city of about forty-three thousand in light-industrial, central Massachusetts. The fifty-four-year-old Democrat could be characterized as a self-made man, a member of the old guard. A graduate of St. Bernard High School, a parochial school in Fitchburg, he is in the real estate business. Lombard is one of the most senior members of the House, having been elected to twelve consecutive terms since 1946. He can be counted on to argue the conservative side of most questions. He is almost always present for roll calls.

The organizations Lombard belongs to reflect his views. He belongs to the Knights of Columbus, the American Legion, VFW, AMVETS, Reserve Officers Assn., Eagles, and Elks. Lombard is a man Spiro Agnew would love if Lombard were a Republican. Lombard takes a strict view toward youth. When the Fitchburg State College student newspaper printed an issue Lombard considered obscene, Lombard and the college president produced a Bill to make all extracurricular activities in every state college subject to the direction of the president.

Such a law, of course, would make the presidents of the state colleges even more subservient to the Legislature, from which cometh their help and staff and new buildings. The Legislature has a record of being unsympathetic to rebellious students, and the Lombard Bill brought a predictable outcry from the students. "Because I filed that Bill," Lombard told the House one day, "I've got a bunch of nit-wit students running a candidate against me."

Lombard was the wrong man to be chief opposition spokesman, but he was the one who wanted to do it. The opposition spokesman should have been a constitutional lawyer who could have mounted some very strong legal arguments against the Bill on that first day of debate on March 12. If that had been the case, the six-vote margin of victory that day might have been turned into a defeat, and the entire course of the Bill might have changed. Those arguments did not develop. Lombard emphasized that the Bill gave "aid and comfort to the enemy" and that it would be exploited by Communist propagandists. Many opponents asserted that the Bill was unconstitutional because the state had no right to legislate on "foreign policy."

The most dramatic point in the debate, which began at 2 p.m., came at 4:30. The galleries of the House were packed with young people watching the very lively, if not erudite, debate. It was an effort for them to restrain themselves from booing some of the opponents and applauding when Shea or Kiernan made a point. One of the youngest representatives, twenty-eight-year-old Peter C. McCarthy of Peabody, got up to speak. Ironically, the youthful McCarthy, who still looks young enough to be a college student, was opposed to the Bill which the youths in the galleries were so eager to see pass. McCarthy is a former teacher who is a student of politics and boasts "the biggest library of political biographies in Essex County."

McCarthy told the House that men were dying in Vietnam while in Massachusetts people were playing "political games" with the Bill. He said he was concerned that the Bill would raise false hopes among parents that their sons wouldn't have to go to war and that it would be "a cruel hoax" on families of GI's serving in Vietnam. He knew what those families had gone through. John McCarthy, his brother, had been killed in action in Vietnam, February 20, 1967.

Representative McCarthy's restrained but dramatic recounting of his brother's death in Vietnam was the kind of personal, emotional statement that can turn a debate around. Everyone knew on that Thursday that the vote was going to be close, but it stood a fair chance of getting initial approval.

McCarthy had the House in the palm of his hand. This reporter felt at that minute that McCarthy had turned it around, that the uncommitted representatives were going with him. The personal story of one of the more than forty thousand individual tragedies—of lives cut short by the Vietnam war—seemed then as if it might defeat a Bill designed to test whether those lives were lost for an unconstitutional cause.

Connie Kiernan, "the Silver Fox," the chairman of the Judiciary Committee, rose. Speaker Bartley pounded his gavel, cutting off McCarthy. "For what purpose does the gentleman rise?" asked Bartley. "Will the gentleman yield?" said Kiernan in a commanding tone. McCarthy, a freshman legislator, yielded, and the emotional tension of McCarthy's speech was broken. An aide to Speaker Bartley said afterwards, "McCarthy was swaying votes. That's why Kiernan had to stop him."

It was the generation gap in reverse, with the fifty-two-year-old Kiernan defending the rights of youth against the attack by the youthful legislator.

Kiernan skillfully attempted to turn the sympathy of the legislators away from the loyal young Democrat who had lost his brother in Vietnam by reminding the representatives of their legislative loyalties. "When the gentleman accuses your Judiciary Committee of fostering 'a cruel hoax,' " said Kiernan, "I feel compelled to object." Kiernan then reiterated his main point throughout the debate: that a citizen should have the right to petition a court on a grievance against his government, and that the Bill was the only way this could be done for a citizen who was asked to risk his life in an undeclared war. Kiernan, having halted the rhetorical momentum of McCarthy, then let his younger colleague resume. McCarthy knew he had lost the debate. "It taught me a very useful lesson," he said later. "Never yield when things are going your way."

The second roll-call was on a motion by Gerry Lombard to kill the Bill by referring it to the next annual session of the Legislature. It was the crucial vote. Speaker Bartley did not usually stroll along the aisles, chatting to members. But he did it that Thursday, lobbying for the Shea Bill.

The vote was close. To the galleries, the press corps, and the representatives, it looked almost equal as the representatives voted by switching on the green or red lights next to their names on the two electronic voteboards that flank the podium in the huge, elliptical chamber.

Of the 170 Democrats, only 89—four more than half—voted for the Bill. Sixteen of the 20 Republicans who had voted on the first roll-call against referring the Bill to Attorney General Quinn, thereby keeping the Bill alive, again voted on the second roll-call to keep the Bill alive. Eleven other Republicans joined them.

House Clerk Wallace C. Mills announced the vote in his monotonous, nasal tone: "On this matter, 110 having voted in the affirmative, 116 in the negative, this matter is *not* referred to the next annual session."

The galleries cheered and applauded as Speaker Bartley pounded the gavel. The first round was over. Twenty representatives had had their say for 3½ hours. On a voice vote, House Bill 5165 was given initial approval, and John Wells left the gallery smiling. "I never thought we'd really make it, even when I thought we had the votes," he said. "But we've got a way to go yet." The 116 votes the Bill received was not a majority of the House, which had 238 members and two vacancies at that time. One hundred twenty votes were essential to ensure that the 12 representatives who had failed to vote could not be persuaded to kill the Bill.

Using Pressure

The pressure, public and private, was on. Speaker Bartley issued a public statement that, "as Speaker of the Massachusetts House of Representatives, I am personally pleased that this legislative body has dared to start the process" of a Bill which "will force the United States Supreme Court to decide whether or not Congress's right to declare war has been assumed by the President."

Shea also issued a statement in answer to charges that the Bill was unconstitutional. "Through over six hours of testimony before the Joint Committee on the Judiciary February 11, 1970, several of the nation's outstanding constitutional lawyers testified that: (1) The Constitutionality of the measure could only be determined by the federal courts; (2) The Bill is constitutional under the Massachusetts Constitution; (3) The purpose of the measure is to test the constitutionality of exclusively presidential wars, and the only way to accomplish this act is for the courts to review the constitutionality of the Shea Bill. Thus, even if the Shea Bill is unconstitutional, which by expert testimony it is not, it would still serve the purpose for which it was written, if it were enacted into law.

"It is my firm belief that this measure ought best to be discussed in view of its merits as a method testing the constitutionality of exclusively presidential wars," Shea said.

Other public pressure was exerted through the news media. Shea called a Saturday news conference to announce that twenty legal scholars, including Dr. Hans J. Morgenthau, had sent him telegrams expressing their support of the Bill.

It was an impressive list, and represented an impressive telephone and telegraph bill for Shea, Wells, Worth and others who had carefully solicited the support of each scholar. The Saturday news conference, of course, provided a new reason for the Sunday newspapers to have a story on the Bill and for increased television coverage Saturday night.

Getting Out of Vietnam

With passage of the Bill a real possibility, speculation began on how the Bill might be put into effect. What were the chances of the Bill's actually halting the war? Few, said one of the legal advisors on the Bill. The legal reasoning behind the Bill had not been explained very thoroughly on the floor of the House on Thursday. By 1 a.m. Saturday, this reporter understood why. It took the lawyer about 2½ hours of almost uninterrupted monologue Friday night to detail the many and complex arguments for and against the Bill.

He said that the war might continue even if the Supreme Court ruled favorably that the Vietnam war was unconstitutional. The lawyer noted that the Supreme Court now had ample precedent in the school desegregation case for a gradual implementation of an individual's rights. If the court could allow fifteen years of "all deliberate speed" in implementing the rights of black school children to an equal, desegregated education, it probably could allow the President time to seek a declaration of war from Congress. If the President were unable to obtain a declaration of war from Congress, the court might use the "all deliberate speed" formula to allow the President time to arrange an orderly withdrawal from Vietnam.

The lawyer explained that the legal basis of the Bill was in the constitutions of Massachusetts and the United States. The Bill's legislative title was "An act defining the rights of an inhabitant of the Commonwealth inducted or serving in the military forces of the United States." The legislature's authority to define that right was derived from Part 1, Article X of the Massachusetts Constitution: "Each individual of the society has a right to be protected by it in the enjoyment of his life, liberty and property, according to standing laws." The Bill would extend to the Massachusetts citizen the legal services of the state attorney general, who "shall on behalf of such person, and in the name of the Commonwealth, take all steps he deems appropriate to enforce and defend the rights of such inhabitant."

The assertion of such a right for Massachusetts inhabitants would not be an unconstitutional usurpation of federal authority by state authority, said the lawyer, because the authority is in the federal Constitution under the Fifth Amendment of the United States Bill of Rights. The Fifth Amendment states, "No person shall . . . be deprived of life, liberty or property without due process of law." The "due process" of federal constitutional law provides, under Article I, Section 8 that, "The Congress shall have power . . . to declare war, grant letters of marque and reprisal, and make rules concerning captures on land and water. . . ." On a "strict construction" of the Constitution, it is difficult to argue that the Vietnam war is consistent with due process of law and the citizen's rights, since Congress has made no declaration of war. The only purported link to a declaration of war, the Gulf of Tonkin Resolution which Lyndon Johnson and his Under-Secretary of State, Nicholas deB. Katzenbach, termed a "virtual declaration of war," was repudiated by the Nixon Administration. The repudiation, in the form of a State Department memorandum to Sen. J. William Fulbright, chairman of the Senate Foreign Relations Committee, came on that Friday, the day after the Massachusetts House gave initial approval to the Shea Bill.

The State Department memo, in reference to Fulbright's inquiries regarding the proposed repeal of the Tonkin Gulf Resolution and other resolutions passed at the time of the 1962 Cuban crisis, the 1958 Lebanon crisis, and the 1955 Formosa crisis, stated that the Tonkin Gulf Resolution could no longer be considered as a reason for being in Vietnam. The memorandum was vague on what precise Constitutional authorization was given Nixon for the American involvement in Vietnam. What the justification seemed to be was: We're there because we're there. The State Department memo said: "The administration is not depending on any of these resolutions as legal or constitutional authority for its present conduct of foreign relations or its contingency plans."

The memo also said that the Department intended that Congress "fulfill its proper role under the Constitution in the decision-making process" in the event of new emergencies. The same message was given Fulbright in person by Secretary of State William P. Rogers on April 29, the day before the President announced, without consulting Congress, the American invasion of Cambodia.

The State Department memo released March 13 had not said definitely that the Administration would seek a declaration of war from Congress in the event of new emergencies. If Johnson's Tonkin Gulf Resolution had no relevance to Nixon's Vietnam policy, then, apparently, the United States was fighting the war in Vietnam because we already were in Vietnam. This appeared to be the Nixon rationale in his emphasis, in the early summer of 1970, on modifying the Cooper-Church amendment in Congress so that the "power of the President of the United States to protect American forces" would not be jeopardized in Cambodia. It was difficult to understand his concern, since the Cooper-Church amendment specifically stated: "Nothing contained in this section shall be deemed to impugn the constitutional power of the President as Commander-in-Chief, including the exercise of that constitutional power to protect the lives of United States Armed Forces wherever deployed."

The Constitution does not specifically give the President that power. All that it says, in Article II, Section 2, is: "The President shall be Commander-in-Chief of the army and navy of the United States, and of the militia of the several states when called into the actual service of the several states." What has given the President that power is the gradual accumulation of power through the presidential assumption of power in scores of so-called emergency situations. But none of these emergency situations were quite like the heavy military involvement of the United States in Vietnam from 1965 to 1970.

These were the arguments presented by the lawyer. These same arguments were buttressing hundreds of phone calls that weekend to key legislators.

Old Politics, New People

What turned a narrow six-vote margin of victory on March 12 into a forty-seven-vote margin on March 16 was old politics practiced by new people. It was lobbying by telephone. Representatives were called by people they knew and by people who were strangers. The strangers often called them two or three times to make it seem as though more people were behind the Bill. The Bill's new citizen lobbyists told of one representative who received at least forty-five telephone calls. He switched to supporting the Bill on Monday, the sixteenth, but claimed he had gotten only three calls about the Bill. "Those forty-five calls were only the ones we recorded as going to him," said an organizer of the telephone lobbying effort. "We gave his name out to scores more, who may have called him. One woman said she called him up three times."

When a politician was considered to be more effective than a citizen lobbyist, a politician was used. Congressman Michael Harrington of Salem, who had won a special election on the peace issue, called up the man who had replaced him in the Massachusetts Legislature and convinced him to switch his vote. The citizens' lobby over the weekend was later described by John Wells as "massive." Leading the organization were members of the Citizens for Participation Politics and Mass. PAX (the Massachusetts peace group which initiated the idea of Moratorium Day, October 15, 1969). CPP had been lobbying legislators on the Shea Bill for a long time. A CPP newsletter of February 21, ten days after the hearing on the Shea Bill, published the office and home phones of every member of the Joint Committee on the Judiciary and told its readers; "It is not too late to urge members of the Committee to vote for a favorable report on the Bill."

The votes were switching under this onslaught of phone calls, but there were still moments of suspense to come. Debate on the Shea Bill resumed at 2:05 p.m. on Monday, March 16. Reversal attempts were made in the House to add amendments, which proponents feared would muddy the waters; but the Bill finally passed 136-89. From the turmoil of the House, the Bill went to the Senate where it consistently won 33-6 margins, but not without considerable discussion.

By the time the Bill had passed the House it was beginning to get some national attention. Chairman J. William Fulbright of the Senate Foreign Relations Committee commented, after the 136-89 vote of passage on March 16, "I offer my compliments to the great Commonwealth of Massachusetts. It is showing great leadership." It was clear that the peace issue was going to be a large factor in the Fall elections, and senators were becoming more receptive to the pressure tactics exerted by Shea, Wells, Worth, and their organization. Some of the most conservative (and occasionally obdurate) senators voted for the Bill to the surprise of the State House press gallery. About five to eight Democratic votes could be attributed to Donahue. About three to five of the seven Republican votes for the Bill could be attributed to the volume of support generated by peace groups in behalf of the Bill. The support of the Bill by these seven Republicans—Senators Oliver F. Ames of Boston, James DeNormandie of Lincoln, George Hammond of Westfield, Allen F. Jones of Barnstable, Fred I. Lamson of Malden,

Ronald C. MacKenzie of Burlington, and John M. Quinlan of Norwood—made it more difficult for Sargent to veto the Bill. Senate Minority Leader John Parker of Taunton commented, "Some of the supporters of this Bill went from hawks to doves overnight."

Parker had led the opposition in the Senate, which saw a much more scholarly level of debate than had prevailed in the House. Sen. William L. Saltonstall of Manchester, son of former United States Sen. Leverett Saltonstall, traced briefly the history of military moves by presidents and asserted that such flexibility of action was necessary. Saltonstall knew well the strength of the peace movement. He had been beaten in the previous November in a special Congressional election by a peace candidate, State Rep. Michael Harrington, a Salem Democrat.

A Political Mistake

When the Bill finally went to Governor Sargent, speculation ran wild as his decision was awaited. The various and technical mistakes made in drawing up a final version of the Bill were nothing to the political mistake made by the Democrats. They thought they had Governor Sargent trapped. When Senator Ward was asked in early March about the Bill's potential as a partisan political issue, he told *Boston Globe* reporter Robert L. Turner, "This may be a Bill in which Sargent can't win no matter what he does, if we get it to his desk."

Sargent played coy all the way, refusing to commit himself until the day he signed the Bill. He considered all the options. Veto would have been political suicide. Liberal young Republicans of the Ripon Society had issued a public letter to the governor on March 23, when the Bill first passed the Senate, calling on him to sign it. They told Sargent that questions of the Bill's constitutionality should be resolved in the courts, not in the governor's office. Furthermore, all the potential Democratic candidates for governor—Kenneth O'Donnell, Maurice Donahue, and Boston Mayor Kevin H. White—had endorsed the Bill. Sargent had reservations about the Bill, questioning whether the state was legislating on what was properly a federal matter. Legal opinion was divided. Sargent, therefore, could hardly veto the Bill with a message saying it was clearly unconstitutional. The governor also considered allowing the Bill to become law without his signature.

Finally, Sargent made the decision he had to make as a politician seeking liberal votes in November. He signed the Bill and won the headlines in the national press, which at last had gotten around to covering the issue. Sargent added the emergency preamble at the request of Shea.

The Shea Bill became law with Sargent's signature at 2:15 Thursday afternoon, April 2, 1970.

Fed Up with the War

Whatever the motivations, political or idealistic, behind the Bill, it had become law. That was important regardless of whether the Supreme Court ruled the Vietnam war was constitutional.

The new Massachusetts statute was truly remarkable. What it said, in essence, was that if the President, the Congress, and the Supreme Court declined to mind the Constitutional store, at least one member of the republic of the fifty united states will try to make them adhere to the compact that established a new government in 1787.

"It almost doesn't matter what happens now," said an aide to Speaker Bartley. "By itself, it's the greatest protest yet against the war." That assessment was substantiated by the rapidity with which the Shea Bill became an issue in other states. Former Supreme Court Justice Arthur Goldberg, a Democratic cnadidate for governor in New York State, said he would sign the Bill if it were presented to him as governor. The Bill was introduced in many other states, forcing politicians to take a stand on it.

The Shea Bill passed the Massachusetts Legislature because of a receptive political environment. Basic to that environment was a nation that was exasperated by the Vietnam war. For nearly two years, according to the Gallup Poll, more than half the American people had believed the United States had made a mistake sending troops to Vietnam. In August, 1968, 53 per cent of those polled thought it was a mistake; in March, 1969, 52 per cent. A three-day nationwide Gallup Poll that was started April 3, the day after Sargent signed the Shea Bill, found that 51 per cent of Americans considered the war a mistake.

The strength of anti-war sentiment was evident. Not once was a voice raised during the legislative debate in defense of the war. No one urged stepping up the war against Hanoi.

The Shea Bill probably never would have passed without these strictly political pre-conditions: (1) a Democratic-dominated state legislature partisanly eager to embarrass a Republican governor and a Republican president; (2) the House cut issue, which embarrassed the legislature and further heightened their desire to embarrass Sargent; (3)

39

the intention of Senate Pres. Maurice Donahue to run for governor against Sargent.

Even with these pre-conditions, however, there was no guarantee that the Bill would pass. Jim Shea told the House on March 12 that he did not think he had a single vote among the Judiciary Committee before the hearing. His Bill, however, caught the imagination of legal experts, legislators, and the press, and excellent legal arguments convinced the Judiciary Committee at the hearing. Shea played a major role as the middleman and coordinator between the eager citizens' lobby and the legislators. He proved himself to be one of the most effective liberal representatives in the House.

The citizens' lobby worked hard and effectively to develop the Bill and to switch some votes, and Bartley and Donahue worked hard along the same lines, for similar and dissimilar reasons.

It was the old politics, practiced superbly for a new cause and for a multitude of reasons. One legislator, who had been active in behalf of the Bill and on behalf of the League of Women Voters' petitions to cut the size of the House, gave an indication of the political maze. He said at a victory party, April 3; "The League of Women Voters, that's who passed the Bill." It was a purposely exaggerated comment, but there was some truth behind it. Passage of the Shea Bill had been no simple task.

4

A Young Man of Lexington

Daniel Small

For several years before the spring of 1970, millions of Americans had been searching for a real, meaningful way to put an end to a war they thought was immoral and illegal. I was one of them. In 1968, I worked as student coordinator of the Eugene McCarthy campaign in Lexington, Massachusetts, and then spent one of the most agonizing, heartwrenching, and depressing weeks of my life in front of a TV set watching my hopes—and the hopes of all of us who had worked so hard for McCarthy—go down the drain in the disgusting spectacle that was the Chicago Convention. In the Fall of that year I joined a number of other Lexington students to work for a "peace" candidate for state representative. Eventually, I also worked for Vice-President Humphrey, making a choice between the "lesser of two evils." But a busy Fall of canvassing, leafleting, telephoning, fund-raising, and high hopes came to an end with defeat in the November elections for both of the candidates for whom we had worked so hard.

My political action continued, though, with work for Citizens for Participation Politics (CPP), as one of the founders and leaders of 18 X 72—an organization working to lower the voting age in Massachusetts to eighteen by 1972, and even in Lexington High School—as an unsuccessful candidate for President of the Class of 1971. In August of 1969, I was one of those fortunate enough to go to Woodstock; I say fortunate because Woodstock was more than a festival. It was the coming together, literally and figuratively, of hundreds of thousands of young people and a reaffirmation of themselves and of their common goals of peace and love. It was one of the most meaningful experiences in my life, and I came back to Lexington with new faith in my generation and what we could do. It was not long after I came back that I met John Wells.

The war was continuing, Nixon had not lived up to his campaign promises, and our troops were still dying in this immoral, illegal war. Many Lexingtonians, therefore, joined with millions of others nationwide in wanting to express their concern on the October 15 Moratorium. With the help of Reverend Wells—without whom October 15 and most of Lexington Peace Action's efforts would not have been nearly so successful as they were—students and adults met, leafleted, telephoned, raised funds, and did everything they could to bring people out on October 15. They were successful. Almost one thousand high school students stayed out of school in Lexington; and while two other students and myself spoke on a radio talk show, hundreds of Lexington citizens, mostly students, canvassed the entire town with anti-war petitions. In the afternoon five thousand people came to the Lexington Green to show their concern and to hear Governor Sargent—whom John Wells was instrumental in bringing to the Green—and other speakers denounce the war in Vietnam.

All this work, yet what had it accomplished? Very little. The news media spent most of its time on ten or twenty high school students, who admitted they were there only to get on TV and to disrupt the rally with shouts of "Kill, kill, kill!" Yet would it have mattered anyway? The petitions, with thousands of names, including the governor's, were sent to our congressman to be delivered to the President, but we knew they would have no real effect. As for the rally itself, five thousand people are too easily forgotten, and forgotten they were. October 15 went better than we had dreamed, but it had little effect.

Something had to be done, so we made plans for slightly different activities in November. Our first meeting, planned largely by John Wells, was later followed by a series of hearings on the subject held by Sen. Edward Kennedy throughout the state. The first hearing was held in Lexington. Further study and work on the problem is still going on. Next we helped sponsor a meeting in Lowell with our congressman, who came at the invitation of Reverend Wells. Finally we sent two rental buses with students to participate in the mass rally in Washington on November 15, 1969.

Again there was so much work, but what were the results? Both of our meetings were sparsely attended, but even an overflow crowd could not stop the war. The March on Washington, though a good and interesting experience, did little. President Nixon said he would not be affected, and even though he was affected he did not really listen and did not respond. Hundreds of thousands were almost as easily forgotten as five thousand would have been.

The question was, "What next?" and it was with this question on my mind that I walked into John Wells's office as I had become accustomed to doing. It was early December, and I wanted to tell him of my election as Massachusetts Student Government Day Representative from Lexington High School. On this day, which was to be on April 3, 1970, high school students from all over the state "take over" the State House and act on bills introduced by the students. As I came into John's office, I was already planning to file several bills, including one to lower the voting age and one for drug education. As it turned out, three of the six bills the Student Government considered had my name on them and all three passed. John handed me a suggested bill, which turned out to be the Shea-Wells Bill, and asked me for my opinion. This was to be the third of my bills that the Student Government passed.

For years those against the war, myself included, have been calling it illegal and immoral. Yet somehow, largely because we felt there was nothing we could do about the former, it was the latter that had always been emphasized. Because of the feeling that the war was immoral, that the system was not doing anything to stop an illegal war, many individuals turned away from the system, some of them violently. But the system was not at fault. The Constitution clearly makes the war in Indochina illegal, but individuals were ignoring this fact. What John Wells handed me that afternoon was an "impossible dream," a chance to right the wrongs caused by years of senseless unconstitutional war.

I filed the bill for consideration by the Student Government, before it was introduced to the actual Legislature; but Student Government Day became an almost trivial affair for the future, as the next few months became lost in a blur of activity, as we did everything we could humanly do to make the "impossible dream" come true. I truly cannot remember everything I did on "the Bill" as we called it. One of the first things was leading a busload of Lexington students into the press conference at which the Bill's introduction was announced. After that came planning, leafleting, fund-raising, and then leading two busloads of students into the hearing before the Judiciary Committee. The Chairman, Senator Ward, later told us that he was "overwhelmed and convinced" that after the hearing, we were working to win.

Amid all this work, I had the real pleasure of meeting Representative Shea several times. He struck me from the start as a dedicated and wonderful man. I will always be glad I had the privilege of working with him, if only for a short time.

After the hearing, our pace only increased. We continued to canvass, leaflet, raise funds, attend meetings, talk, and plan everything possible that might help the Bill. By this time I was writing a column for the local paper, and I used this as much as I could to promote the Bill. We all worked to exhaustion and then worked some more, particularly John Wells. But none of us thought twice about it, because all of us realized the potential importance of the Bill and the good it could do.

On April 3, 1970, Student Government Day, I talked to Mr. René Bouchard, the man in charge of the Day from the Department of Education. He said, "It was too bad" the governor had signed the Bill before the students had time to influence his decision. I agreed with him, but laughed inwardly at how he could call the governor's signing it "too bad."

Few of us will forget that last week leading up to the Bill's passage. The tension, the excitement, the hope, the joy of the fulfillment of a dream are not soon forgotten. At a celebration party that weekend John remarked to me that he had never seen so much joy in one room; I hadn't either. It was a joy that we had won, but it was more than that. It was a joy that all was not lost, that the system had responded and that maybe, just maybe, we had helped bring this horrible war to an end.

Finally, there were a lot of people who helped with the Bill. The list of students, parents, legislators, legal experts, and everyone else is endless. But of all the names that will be associated with the Bill, of all the names that will be used, the names of Jim Shea and John Wells can never be used too often. Without these two great men, there would have been no Bill, and every one of us owes them a great debt of gratitude.

5   Random Notes from a Lawyer

Lawrence Adler

In the fall of 1969, Rev. John Wells had spoken with me a number of times as to what might be done legally to test the validity of the *de facto* war then going on only in Vietnam. He hoped thereby to attempt to show the youth of the country that the legal system would have some relevance to the functioning of government in this area and also possibly to have an inhibitive effect on any possible expansion of the war. As a lawyer, I flinched both visibly and mentally when the question came up of the utilization of a state as a lever in this endeavor; I remembered the demise of the mid-nineteenth century doctrine of interposition and nullification which had been used to defend slavery, and which had been disinterred since 1954 in an attempt to prevent or at least delay the carrying out of the constitutional mandate of desegregation in the public schools of the nation.

However, after several protracted discussions, I came to appreciate the distinction between using a state's law to *deprive* its inhabitants of their rights under the federal Constitution, as had been historically done too many times, and using the state's law-making power affirmatively to *secure* rights of its citizens guaranteed under the Constitution. Once this differential was articulated and understood by us, it required a relatively short time for John and me to draft the petition that subsequently became known as the "Shea–Wells Bill".

In early December, 1969, John Wells stopped in to see me at my law office one busy day and asked me if I could give him the necessary time to work with him in drafting such a Bill. In effect we were setting up a confrontation between state law and federal officials to test the validity of the Vietnam war by seeking a judicial determination of the nature and extent of the powers granted to the President as Commander-in-Chief under the United States Constitution.

We drafted the Bill in more or less short order and avoided any problems that we thought might result from attempting to limit the discretion of the state attorney general by requiring legal action *via* the original jurisdiction of the Supreme Court of the United States. In retrospect, I know that I had practically no hope that the Bill would ever pass the General Court of Massachusetts, and I believe John was of the same frame of mind. However, both of us were of the opinion that it could be a vehicle to inform the electorate of the legal issues rarely discussed in the whole tragedy. Of course, each of us had a secret hope that maybe this *was* in fact an idea whose time had come and one which would prove, therefore, irresistible: but I would be less than candid to say that this was more than a hope in the background at that point.

After my secretary typed the petition, John left with it to talk with Kenneth P. O'Donnell and other officials whose positions were basically the same as ours and attempt to find a representative who would introduce the petition for us. We had drafted it on the form for the House of Representatives simply because it was more likely that we could find a representative to introduce it rather than one of the less numerous state senators. Neither of us had any real idea as to who would introduce it, and we both recognized that we had a very limited time to meet the filing deadline for the introduction of new Bills in the General Court.

Several times during the next few weeks, I asked John what had happened to our Bill. Each time he told me he had a representative from Newton who would introduce the Bill "upon request," but that he didn't know whether the Bill was actually in the hopper and we would just have to wait and see what had happened to it. One day John told me that he had learned that the Bill had in fact been filed and that the representative, H. James Shea, Jr., had become convinced of the merit of the Bill and would now actively sponsor it in the House.

Thereafter, we met several times in give-and-take skull sessions with other people of a similar frame of mind, such as Profs. Steve Worth and Larry Velvel. We had like sessions discussing both the constitutional *merits* of the bill and the pros and cons of various *procedures* proposed by interested people who were familiar with the legislative techniques for presenting a Bill in its most favorable light. The consensus resulted in a most unusual public hearing from the Joint Committee of the General Court in February of 1970. At this hearing an outstanding list of speakers was produced, and I believe that their presentation convinced a number of the members of the Joint Committee to actively support the Bill.

When the Bill came out of the Committee, a number of changes had been made in it procedurally pertaining to what the attorney general was to do under the Bill; but the basic ideas that John and I had agreed on in the original draft were unchanged, and this pleased us both very much since we felt that the Bill had not in any way been watered down nor the basic question it presented made obscure.

Thereafter, John and Assistant Atty. Gen. Bob Condlin and I met several Saturdays at our Unitarian Church in Lexington where we pored over various redrafts suggested by different influential members of the House and Senate; and, while attempting to meet their suggestions, we managed to preserve the basic structure of the substantive portion of the Bill intact. I believe that the Bill which finally came forth with a substantial approval from the Joint Committee was basically the Bill that we finally agreed upon.

Shortly afterwards the voting started, and I was then an eyewitness to how participation politics by ordinary citizens can function effectively. Throughout the Commonwealth, ordinary citizens did, as we are so often exhorted to do, get in touch with their representatives and senators and urge adoption of the Bill. In fact, I was one of a delegation from Lexington who met with our own state representative and had some part in causing him to cease opposition to the Bill.

Naturally, when the Bill was finally adopted after all the interim votes, I was thrilled with what had been accomplished by so few in such a short time and was delighted to host a celebration in honor of the occasion on April 3, 1970.

As a follow-up, I participated with Steve Worth and Larry Velvel at my office in the drafting of a short form of petition for the general public to sign urging a judicial hearing on the Bill on Massachusetts' litigation thereunder, along with a short question-and-answer sheet that

John Wells, Jim Shea, and I had worked out at my home some weeks earlier for distribution to the public to attempt to clear away some of the doubts raised by opponents of the Bill.

All in all, it was a most stimulating, interesting and, hopefully, worthwhile experience. Now let the system prove it actually works.

6   High School Involvement

Lee Goldstein

About five minutes past two on Thursday afternoon, April 2, Barbara (Billie) Nelson telephoned me in my home-room at Saugus High School. The governor had just signed OUR Bill. She had stayed out of school that day and had seen it with her own eyes—the culmination of seven weeks of intense, inspiring, rewarding, and frustrating work. Until this week we had been on a staggered school session that allowed us to be at the State House by 1:30. A few minutes later Faye called. She had seen the signing on TV. Then Ronnie called. Tommy rushed back to school to be sure I knew, and I ran down to the visual-aids room to get a recap on the radio. Ordinarily, I would have brought a portable radio to school. However, I was absolutely sure that the governor would wait until at least Monday to do anything about our Bill.

OUR Bill! We wanted this Bill passed—H2396 we called it, though our H2396 buttons were covered with adhesive tape sporting the new number H5165. The success of OUR Bill meant the efficacy of telephone calls, letters, and public information meetings offered in good faith with the sole purpose of educating people. At 2:05 p.m. on April 2, we felt that hard work, truth, education, and sincerity could influence those in power. We had seen how our state government works, and this time we weren't disappointed. Certainly at times during the interminable debates in both the House and the Senate when we heard much blind rhetoric from many who we felt had not done their homework, we were discouraged. When my own representative stood up and impugned the motives of those supporting OUR Bill, when my girl friend's representative sent her, in response to a letter giving her reasons for support of OUR Bill, an American flag decal with the inscription "Love it or Leave," we were discouraged. We know that some representatives voted for or against the Bill for pragmatic political reasons without weighing the merits of the proposed legislation, but we feel that the result represented a victory for the forces of informed reason.

I first heard of this Bill in December, 1969. Louis Lyons mentioned that a Bill to test the constitutionality of undeclared wars had been introduced in the House of Representatives by H. James Shea, Jr. of Newton. I remember being tickled that it was Jim, a friend of mine from ski-country, who had the guts to introduce something that was bound to be controversial. On January 29 Jim discussed the "undeclared war" Bill with Louis Lyons on the WGBH news. I felt then that the Bill was interesting and it was good for some healthy discussion and perhaps a demonstration, and I decided at least to attend the public hearing on February 11.

Betsy and Paul, two of my students, asked me Wednesday morning February 11, if I were by any chance going to the State House for the public hearing of the so-called "undeclared war Bill." We drove together to the subway station where I left my car. We got to the State House just after two, and to our surprise and pleasure the hearing was just getting underway. It had been scheduled for a small room in the morning. But since a huge crowd of spectators was present, the committee had had to reschedule it to the auditorium, which was in session in the morning, so we didn't miss anything. I'm not sure what Betsy and Paul expected, but I know I had simply come to be counted. I was not aware at the time that this Bill was a serious effort to remedy an evil. I thought it simply represented an opportunity to demonstrate against the war with a gimmick—"the undeclared war." Though I am generally considered among my friends to be an optimistic person, I think I had begun to feel a kind ot impotence. One could demonstrate and hope to be noticed by a few people, but not by too many. However, as a whole, our demonstrations were relegated to the streets; we would be heard by our friends only, and the President would make no attempt to communicate to us as he catered to his silent majority. The "why we are in Vietnam" explanation of November 3 along with the buses barricading the White House on November 15 affected me, I think, more than I had realized, because I came to this hearing merely to be counted and not really thinking that anybody could do anything.

What a hearing! Gardner auditorium was mobbed upstairs and downstairs; people were standing in the aisles. There was a group of men who seemed quite disinterested—relaxed, yawning; they were the members of the Joint House-Senate Committee of the Judiciary with Senator Ward of Fitchburg presiding. After Jim introduced the Bill, a member of the committee asked whether the President didn't have the power to deploy troops as a result of the Tonkin Gulf Resolution. Jim said that he could give his own opinion but that he had a much more authoritative person available to testify. "Oh, we have confidence in you, Representative Shea," said a member of the committee. Eventually, a wise-looking, white-haired little man stood up to explain the Tonkin Gulf Resolution. He was former Senator Gruening of Alaska, one of the two senators who had voted against the Resolution. He said that the senators who voted on the Resolution had done so under the impression that they were granting the power to act in a temporary emergency situation, not that they were giving blanket power to act. For more than four hours I listened to speeches and answers from people of this calibre—constitutional law professors from all over the country. I was particularly moved by our own Prof. Steven Worth of Northeastern University who pleaded for action within the system. The hearing was fun, too—all those law professors and politicians extolling the soil of Massachusetts "where the shot was fired heard round the world," etc. Why shouldn't the grand old revolutionary state of Massachusetts lead the nation as it had done against the tyranny of George III? And an amazing thing was happening. I had the feeling that just as I was becoming involved and excited by these speeches, so were many of the men on the Committee of the Judiciary.

They were asking serious questions of the witnesses who were foreign policy and constitutional law experts. Toward the end of the hearing a tiny young woman who seemed very erudite got up to be recorded as a witness in favor of the Bill. She said that this was the first time in several years that she didn't feel ashamed to call herself an American. She hoped that the committee would look favorably on the Bill and that she would have the opportunity to work for it. Senator Ward wanted to know whether she would drop out again if they voted against it, and whether she didn't feel that this was a "sour grapes" kind of attitude—you support the system when it is working for you and you reject it when you don't get your way. She then explained that her disillusionment was caused by the assassinations and politics of repression of these last few years. This would simply be a last straw. She said it all much better than I could have. In the next seven weeks I saw a lot of Robin Remington, Research Assistant at M.I.T. She was to be a valuable speaker for the Bill at many public meetings.

The hearing finally ended and Betsy, Paul, and I went downstairs. I introduced them to my friend Jim; and they introduced me to Rev. John Wells, whom they had met through Paul's summer camp experience and through working for the October Moratorium. My Winthrop neighbor, Simon Fitch, was there too, and we all took the subway together, after he bought us chocolate bars. I'm mentioning all these people now because they formed the nucleus of those with whom I worked for passage of this Bill. We ate the chocolate bars on Tremont Street, Boston, and practically danced to the subway station, we were so exhilarated. We had listened to five hours of intelligent speeches and questions and answers. I didn't know where to go from there but my immediate reaction was, other people have to have this opportunity. This is right. We should be able to discuss the war and related problems in public places with publicly elected officials. We should not be kicked into the streets. I would work to give the people in my community the opportunity to hear intelligent people discuss the questions of the undeclared war in a public place moderated by a public official—on a smaller scale, of course, than the hearing just completed.

The next day I called Reverend Wells. He told me he would be happy to speak for his Bill anytime and anywhere and that he would get other speakers. A hearing for the public, moderated by an elected public official in a public place, is what I wanted. I called my local representative at the State House and asked him if he would moderate. He was involved in other issues, supported the President all the way, and did not see this issue as I did. I then called my state senator. He accepted, making it clear that he would be an impartial moderator. He hoped to hear all sides of the proposed legislation, and he did not wish to be put on the spot by his constituents. The idea again was to have a public debate, on a question of public interest, in a public place, moderated by an elected public official. This would be, in a sense, telling Vice-President Agnew that intelligent critical discussion was not un-American. My senator, I felt, had every right at this stage of the legislation to come as an impartial moderator for the purpose of further informing himself as well as informing us. He could make his decision in a few weeks when the legislation reached the Senate, if it did. He warned me that the effort to inform others might be futile if the Bill were to be reported out of committee in a week as mentioned at the hearing. It was Saturday, February 14, that I spoke to my senator. The Bill could conceivably be reported out on Tuesday the seventeeth and be brought before the House on Wednesday the eighteenth. If it was voted down there, it was dead for this session.

What to do? Work for the public meeting or work to get an affirmative vote on the Bill in the House? At this point it seemed to me much more important to hold public meetings on this Bill, because these would be discussions of the war as well as the Constitution. Besides, only a few representatives had been at the public hearing on February 11. Were they informed enough to vote in favor of the Bill? It seemed that the wise line of action would be to try to persuade the Committee on the Judiciary to hold the Bill up for a few weeks. So I tried. Between February 11 and February 20 I wrote three letters to Chairman Ward.

I first wrote to Senator Ward and other members of his Committee immediately after the February 10 hearing to tell them how I felt about the Bill in the hope that it would be reported out favorably. In a letter dated Saturday, February 14, I told him about my planned public hearing. I asked him if it would be possible to hold the Bill in committee for a few weeks. I wrote:

> This would give me and, I imagine, many other individuals time to encourage healthy discussion about it. It is not a road Bill that one would want to kill or pass in order to prohibit or start construction immediately, and I feel that discussion of Presidential powers, whether or not one approves of what the President is doing with them, is healthy discussion of our form of government. Holding the Bill up in Committee a few weeks would serve as an incentive for healthy community discussion of a rather academic but important issue—our form of government, our Constitution.

On Sunday the fifteenth, my girlfriend Dorothy and I drove up to Cannon Mountain during a blizzard. We had a lot of time to think and discuss while driving, and when we got settled in an inn we decided to spend the stormy late-afternoon hours with the Sunday *Globe*. I read an article by Peter Newman of the *Toronto Star* entitled "A Canadian's Troubled View of Washington" in which he analyzed the mood he had felt on a recent visit to Washington. After interviews with several senators ranging from Gene McCarthy to Strom Thurmond he could sense the disintegration of constitutional democracy in this country. He ended his article by citing a not frequently quoted paragraph of John F. Kennedy: "Before my term is ended, we shall have to test anew whether a nation organized and governed such as ours can endure. The outcome is by no means certain."

The article troubled me and triggered another letter to Senator Ward in which I apolgized for the barrage of letters and explained about the article. I closed with these paragraphs:

> Can a nation such as ours endure? Most of the time I feel and react positively. Sometimes I am skeptical. I think our Bill can act as a built-in safety-valve security system. While the passage of the Bill is hanging over the State legislature, we can debate, shout, scream, protest, and discuss intelligently the proper use of power, the divisions of power established by the Constitution, etc., etc. If the Massachusetts State Legislature should pass the Bill we would be in the position to protest, still from within the system, the structure of the system. This is healthy and American.
>
> I urge you again most sincerely to hold the Bill up a month and during this time lead and encourage discussion on it.

We skied on Monday. On Tuesday I typed up the Bill, left a space, and added this note:

> This Bill was aired at an open hearing in Gardner Auditorium in the Massachusetts State House by members of the State Joint House-Senate Committee of the Judiciary on Wednesday, February 11. If you feel after reading this Bill and Reverend Wells's *Rationale in Support of H2396* that it is worthy of serious discussion and consideration would you write to Senator Ward, Chairman of the House-Senate Committee of the Judiciary, State House, Beacon Hill, Boston, and ask him to hold up consideration of it for a few weeks. If the Committee recommends or withholds recommendation, the Bill will be presented to the Legislature immediately. If it dies, it dies and discussion will not be relevant. If the Committee delays consideration of the Bill we will have time to hold public forums.

I don't know how many letters Senator Ward received asking that the Bill be held up in committee, but I duplicated and distributed about 150 copies of the Bill with my note and Reverend Wells's *Rationale* on Tuesday and Wednesday, February 17 and 18. School was recessed for February vacation, and many of these copies I mailed to fellow teachers. At the March 9 hearing in Saugus, Mrs. Myron Donoghue of the Democratic Women on Wheels, who had been working in Senator Ward's office, sought me out to tell me that the letters had been very effective.

Reverend Wells told me over the weekend that we had gained another week, and we set up Tuesday, March 3, as the date of our hearing. If the Bill were reported out that day it wouldn't matter. An informed audience could let its representatives know its feelings.

On Monday night, February 23, the Winthrop Peace Action Group held a public meeting at which Reverend Virgil Wood spoke on "The Economy of Peace." Between the lecture and the question-and-answer period, the chairman of the meeting announced the public hearing for the following week. Copies of the Bill and *Rationale* were distributed, and my friend Simon circulated a petition in support of the Bill which was sent to Senator DiCarlo.

At the close of that meeting, Simon and I went to Winthrop Town Hall to catch the tail end of the Selectmen's meeting in order to get their permission to use the hearing room in the Town Hall. This turned out to be too small so we settled on the Town Hall Annex, fondly known as The Old Church Building, across the street from the Town Hall. All our publicity stated that a forum on "HB2396, the rights of a Massachusetts citizen inducted or serving in the military forces of the United States" moderated by Senator Joseph DiCarlo would be held on Tuesday evening, March 3, at the WINTHROP TOWN HALL ANNEX (Old Church building). We wanted to emphasize the fact that the war and the government could be debated in public places in the presence of public officials.

We decided to publicize the meeting in the five cities and towns represented by Senator DiCarlo, but we would concentrate on Saugus, where I taught, and Winthrop, where it would be held. My girlfriend and colleague, Jeanne Gallant, wrote letters of invitation to the seven state representatives who reside in the first Suffolk Senatorial District.

Betsy and Paul passed the word around to fellow Saugus students. Flyers went into teachers' mail boxes. Betsy, Paul, Billie Nelson, and Elizabeth Hamilton made posters with "take-one" pockets. These went up during the week in Winthrop. Materials concerning the Bill were distributed to Saugus High School social studies teachers. Press releases were sent to the local papers in each of the five towns. We had to get into Winthrop High School. They have a forum there. The faculty advisor to this group and several of her students distributed flyers, and we put the student-forum chairman on a panel to question the speakers. Another Winthrop student, Ruth Reinstein, was to share the literature and action table with Billie. Ruth's mother, with friends in the Winthrop Peace Action Group, would provide coffee and cake.

So we had a public place, a public official for a moderator, a public Bill in question, the experts to speak about it, publicity, and a literature-action table (petitions, post cards); but we didn't have any opposition, and we sincerely wanted all aspects of the Bill discussed. I asked Larry, Keith, and Paul—politically conservative members of the faculty of my school—if they would prepare an opposition side. They felt that the Bill was unconstitutional, that it was "states' rights," and that it was no question for the State Legislature; but they did not feel qualified to debate the topic with Reverend Wells, who was a lawyer as well as a minister and who had worked in federal-state relations for several years. I asked Paul to prepare the role of devil's advocate and as a last resort he, of course, would have done that. We also called Atty. Joseph Oteri, who often took the conservative position on educational TV's public debate show "The Advocates." He, also, if we became desperate, might have done it, though he didn't feel that he had the time do do the professional job he likes to do. So here we were on Monday morning with many leads but no real commitments to the negative side of the issue, and we had promised to have all sides examined.

Mr. Munelly, former Superintendent of Schools in Saugus, gave us a fine solution—simply question the experts in an intelligent manner, using a panel of responsible loyal opposition, because at this point there could not have been too many people with good arguments against the Bill since few people were even aware of the Bill. HB2396 was just being born. The idea became to listen to the supporters of the Bill and try to understand them, ask them sticky questions, and then make up our minds. Perhaps the first public meeting could create some honest opposition for a second public meeting. Thus we finally established the format for the forum. Mr. Munelly, a teacher of American History, Mr. Tibbetts (opposed to the Bill as he saw it), Paul, and Miss Marlene Rubitsky, chairman of the Winthrop High School Forum, would act as the panel and would ask carefully prepared questions of the experts before opening up the question period to the audience.

On the 6:00 p.m. news, just before the meeting, it had been announced that the Bill would probably be reported out the following week. One of the most exciting things that happened at this public meeting was the same thing that happened to Betsy, Paul, Simon, and me on February 11; a kind of electrical charge went through the audience—a determination that this discussion must be kept alive and that more people should hear it. Several students who attended invited Reverend Wells, Professor Worth, and Miss Remington to speak in Saugus the next Monday. Reverend Wells was not able to make it, but Representative Shea agreed to go. The students, then, had a panel and less than a week to publicize it and get a hall. They succeeded. Their opposition panel included an English teacher from Saugus High School and a Vietnam veteran on leave. They made two thousand flyers and two dozen posters with "take-one" pockets; they called each of the fifty Saugus Town Meeting members and every member of the League of Women Voters, and they hand-delivered invitations to each of the selectmen and school committee members. Their press release appeared in the Saugus column of the *Lynn Item* the day of the meeting. It read:

This meeting, like the one in Winthrop, developed a hard core group of people who kept up the day-to-day work of informing other people. We never missed a day of debate or of voting. Some of us even showed up on days when no action was taken. We carried letters and petitions daily from constituents to members of the legislature and later to the governor. We were useful, we had fun, and we learned a lot.

In the galleries we saw our friends Reverend Wells and his contingent from the Lexington CPP (Citizens for Participation Politics); Fred King, a private citizen who had had H2396 bumper stickers and copies of the Bill printed; Robin with Sharon and Elisabeth from the Beacon Hill Support Group, who distributed the H2396 buttons and were present at each of our meetings and the M.I.T. Anti-War Conference; John and David of Jim's staff; and Professor Worth. My cousin Ellen and Aunt Jo from South Boston and friend Dorothy from Quincy, who had been at the public hearings, were often there as were several of my students and their parents. This is, of course, not to mention the members of various groups as well as individual, interested citizens who came now and then to hear the debates. My contingent, Reverend Wells, the Beacon Hill Support Group, and Jim's staff were always there and looked to each other for encouragement when a vote looked close and went outside to huddle and discuss strategy from time to time. We made up the H2396 family.

H2396 became H5165 when it was reported out of committee favorably on Tuesday, March 10, by a vote of 17 to 0, with a few abstentions. I heard it on the 6:00 p.m. news that day. It was reported out too late to make the Wednesday House calendar for debate, so we had until Thursday to provide strong support. Wednesday and Thursday the Saugus High contingent mustered up a petition stating that the undersigned members of the SHS faculty supported the Bill. A second petition, with only the names of social studies teachers, was also circulated. In addition, students collected letters from parents, friends, and teachers to be handed personally to Representative Bly, along with the petitions.

On Thursday I got permission to leave school immediately after my last class instead of staying for make-up. Ron's mother came also and drove some of the contingent to Boston. I drove directly up to the State House, let the students out, and double-parked with a policeman's permission. The debates had just started, and I heard the same arguments for and against the Bill that I had heard at our public meetings. Representative Bly, to whom Elisabeth and Jane had delivered the petitions and letters, came upstairs to greet us. He asked if we'd like to be recognized by the chair. This is done as courtesy to the representatives. "The House is pleased to greet Pack 67 Cub Scouts from Saugus with their den mothers," etc. We thanked him and said it wasn't necessary. The debate continued. I got the impression that the representatives were not listening to each other but were mouthing their own arguments.

It disappointed me to hear the representative from the Town of Winchester, Harrison Chadwick, state that he considered this Bill to be "partial secession from the union . . . a willingness to set aside federal law." He evidently had not so much as glanced at Professor Worth's brief, which had been distributed to every representative. I heard that we were attempting to usurp the powers that belong to the Congress of the United States, and I heard over and over in different ways that our enemies in Hanoi would have a heyday with this legislation—that they would use it against our POW's. This has been the basic argument against anti-war demonstrations since 1965: "Hanoi will make propaganda out of it and you're demoralizing the troops in Vietnam."

On the roll-call vote on whether to refer the bill to the next annual session, which was meant to kill it, we all shuddered. There seemed to be many more green kill lights than red "no" lights, but the final count was 116-110 in our favor. In the hallways of the gallery we began to plan our strategy. The students met a representative from Springfield who particularly liked young people, offered us Cokes and ice cream,

58

explained the vote as he saw it, and got us Xeroxed copies of the roll call. Ron's mother had left earlier with some of the contingent. A few with term papers to write or tests to study for took the subway home. George, Elisabeth, and Billie stayed with Simon and me for the strategy session with Jim, his aides, and Professor Worth.

The strategy session took place in an empty hearing room. Monday there would be a vote to reconsider today's vote. Perhaps the governor, if he did not want to be faced with the choice of signing the Bill, might put some pressure on those Republican representatives who had voted with us. We would thank them over the weekend and tell them that we were counting on them to continue to support the Bill. We had decided to call all the representatives who we felt might possibly be persuaded to vote with us on Monday. Certain calls were assigned to certain people. We would ask our friends to deluge the representatives with thank-you calls and support calls, and we would deluge the talk programs over the weekend to keep the debate alive.

On Friday in school, armed with the roll-call vote and a list of faculty names and addresses, I rounded up people to telephone and telegraph their representatives over the weekend. Friday night I made some calls myself. I asked Mr. Everett from school to speak to his friend Representative Chadwick from Winchester. My cousin Ellen would contact her two representatives from South Boston. Miriam, who teaches with me, along with her friends in Methuen would try to win over Representative Buglione. Mrs. Buckner, who also teaches with me, would try to conquer Representative Conway of Malden.

My cousin Ellen's biggest coup was her attack in Salem. Both representatives from Salem (who had replaced very liberal, peace-oriented representatives in a recent special election) had voted against the Bill. Ellen's best friend, recently married, lives in Salem, and her husband had gone to college with one of these new representatives, Mr. O'Donnell. The couple had been vacationing during the week and until Ellen's call had been unaware of Thursday's vote. They contacted both their representatives, who were willing to discuss the bill with a group of constituents. A coffee-hour meeting was held Sunday night at which one of their representatives was won over.

I made at least forty telephone calls myself Saturday and Sunday, and wrote a letter to a certain Mr. Swift, who in the name of the American Legion, was quoted on the 8 a.m. Saturday news as opposing the Bill. It seems he was misquoted, as he immediately answered my letter opting in favor of a court test of the President's war-making powers.

My own representative seemed to listen to me when I spoke to him Saturday afternoon. He gave me his ear for about an hour and let me answer all his objections to the Bill. His major objection that Saturday seemed to be that he doubted the constitutionality of the Bill. After speaking to him, I clarified my point of view in writing, including the list of twenty legal scholars who endorsed the Bill.

As it happened, my efforts were a waste of time in terms of results. I don't say it was a waste of time because he didn't agree with me, but because he had the nerve to stand up on the floor of the House a few days later and say that of the thirteen telegrams he had received over the weekend asking him to reconsider his vote, seven were from known left-wing elements who wanted to "dismantle our society." He also claimed that he had received a letter saying that one could expect such an insensitive vote "from a person of his national origin and faith." Perhaps he did receive a hate letter or two from some cranks. However, I know what kind of letter he received from me and from some of my friends, and we simply tried to give him the facts as we saw them; facts he could have studied in Professor Worth's brief. None of the representatives who are emotionally frightened by communism, who talked about "godless communism" or "aiding and abetting the enemy" seemed capable of hearing the rationale for the Bill.

Nevertheless, our work over the weekend was another glorious victory for the power of reasoning and tenacity. After three hours of the same kind of debate Monday the roll-call boards lit up, and we could tell we had won. The final vote in favor of the Bill was 136 to 89.

While the H2396 (H5165) family was rejoicing outside the galleries, it was informed that just before adjournment a representative had moved that this vote be reconsidered. We thought that it had been done by an enemy of the Bill, but it seems that a proponent had so moved so that the legislation could never again come up for reconsideration. My contingent came back on Wednesday for the reconsideration vote, which was preceded by about an hour's debate of the same calibre we had heard Thursday and Monday.

By now the Saugus contingent knew its job thoroughly. Before we left the State House on Wednesday, the students examined the Senate Chambers and secured a roster of senators. It was distributed to the mailboxes of the teachers at the Junior and Senior high schools. Again teachers were urged to write to their state senators concerning the Bill. Petitions were circulated at home and at school, and letters were collected. The next Monday we heard almost five hours of debate from the gallery of the Senate. The quality of the debate, I felt, was superior to that of the debate in the House. It centered around the ultimate efficacy of the proposed legislation and the motivation of its supporters. The House amendment to limit the attorney general to the prosecution of no more than one case at a time was thrown out in favor of an amendment that would make the test case a "class case"; i.e., the defendant would represent a whole group of citizens in the same circumstances.

Reverend Wells had anticipated that his Bill might be handled in this way. Several times he had cited the Supreme Court case of the *State of Georgia* v. *The Interstate Commerce Commission,* concerning a change in service by the Pennsylvania Railroad that prevented certain citizens of Georgia from the pursuit of their livelihood. The attorney general of Georgia had taken up the case in the name of all the abused citizens. Reverend Wells conceived of a case that might be called "The Commonwealth of Massachusetts v. the Department of Defense," an idea that was very clear to those who initiated the Bill and to those who had followed its progress and supported it from the beginning.

The State Senate passed the Bill on Monday by a vote of 33 to 6 with one member being absent. My senator, who had moderated our public hearing, voted in favor of the Bill. Now we had to wait for the governor's action, which came in our favor, two days later.

This, of course, is not the end of the story. The attorney general must prepare his case, which will probably come before the Supreme Court in October. Nobody knows whether, or how, the court will treat the questions we seek to have resolved.

An overflow crowd gathers at Gardner Auditorium at the State House in Boston to hear opponents of the Vietnam War and support of House Bill 2396 — the Shea-Wells Bill.

7   A Man from Kansas

Lawrence Velvel

I would like to start by saying that I approach these recollections with a really profound sense of loss because of the death of Jim Shea. It seems strange and incomplete that there will be a book published, but without Jim. I didn't know Jim very long. I knew him personally only during the three-day period that I was in Boston working on the Bill, but I thought in that short period I got to know him pretty well.

We spent a great deal of time together, of course, during the three days. We were on a number of radio shows and we spent one evening at a party, drinking beer afterwards until the small hours of the morning. Out of it all I formed a very clear impression of Jim, and I grew tremendously fond of him as a person for whom I had virtually unbounded respect. His integrity and devotion to principle shone through the battles that he was fighting in the political arena. I think that our country has probably suffered a very serious blow in Jim's death, because he surely had a brilliant career ahead of him. Although he was only thirty years old he had already made his political mark, and there is no doubt in my mind that he could have eventually become a national leader. His death was a terrible blow to me, as I know it was also for the people of Massachusetts. We continue to mourn him.

Now let me tell you how I originally found out about the Massachusetts Bill. I was in Chicago on vacation between the Fall and

Spring terms of the school year, visiting my parents, when a phone call came from a Mr. Steve Worth in Boston. I had never heard of Steve Worth and couldn't imagine what the phone call could be about. He explained that a group in Massachusetts believed it was high time to challenge the constitutional legality of the Vietnam war, and he asked me whether I would come to Boston to testify in favor of the proposed Bill. Quite frankly I was delighted. I had been involved in activities pertaining to the war for quite a while and had filed against the government a suit contesting the war. I had also written articles about the war's constitutionality and at the time Steve called had just finished a book on the subject. Therefore, I was very happy to learn about an organized group in Massachusetts, or for that matter anywhere, which was trying to get this burning question settled through the judicial process.

I must admit that I had a few reservations about what the group in Massachusetts was doing, reservations from a legal standpoint that is. There were legal questions involved as to whether a state could validly pass a law pertaining to the legality of war, as to whether a state would have standing to bring suit on the war, and so on. But the issue seemed to me to be so clearly of overriding importance that it was necessary for any legal doubts to be shelved in favor of pursuing the Massachusetts action, and I hoped that persuasive arguments could be made in the courts in favor of that action. Then, of course, the more I thought about what Massachusetts was doing the more arguments I began to muster in its favor, and the more I became convinced that the state was entirely within the law.

Steve asked me whether I knew other people who would testify on some of the legal aspects of the Bill, and I agreed to make a few calls around the country. I rounded up Michael Tigar of UCLA, a very bright guy and a leading figure on the West Coast. He agreed to testify, as did Warren Schwartz, who at that time was visiting at the University of Illinois and had written an article on the constitutional problems connected with the war. All of this occurred approximately two or two and a half weeks before the day scheduled for the hearings.

I was asked to go to Boston a few days in advance of the hearings to appear on radio programs, on evening talk shows, and at meetings organized to answer questions on the legality of the war. As I remember, I arrived on a Monday and was picked up at the airport and taken directly to a radio station by one of Steve Worth's students. There was nobody at the station yet, so we went to my hotel to drop off my bags and then went back to the station. There I met John Wells,

Jim Shea, and Steve Worth. We spoke for a while before the show, which lasted from about 11 to 1:30 or 2 o'clock. I don't remember too much about that particular show, but I was immediately impressed by Wells, Worth, and Shea, all of whom I thought to be tremendously talented, able, and energetic individuals.

As I look back on it, it seems to me the presentation of the Shea Bill was one of those wonderful happenings in which the right people with the right ideas get together at the right time—and in this case in the right state, because of the open-ended method of testimony permitted in the Massachusetts legislature. But the most important elements were the tremendous talent and dedication of Shea, Wells, and Worth. As far as I'm concerned, these three guys were miracle workers; I just can't say enough for them.

I spent part of the next day going over my testimony and then participated in another radio show that evening. This time Michael Tigar joined us. People phoned in questions during the show, and one fellow, who had been in the military, was quite critical of the Bill. He asked whether anybody on the panel, which consisted of Jim, Mike Tigar, Steve, John, and myself, had ever been in the Army. John Wells answered that question because he, of course, had been in the service for quite a while and had been promoted to the rank of Major. He had also been a Defense Department consultant and in general had a long history with the armed services. John described his activities in the military at some length, and when he was through the erstwhile critic somewhat lamely said, "Well, yes sir, Major, you must be right." I don't exactly know how to explain this but it certainly, in this one case anyway, showed a curious, almost automatic response to authority. When this man who had been so antagonistic heard that he was speaking to a Major, he virtually clicked his heels, saluted, and said, "Yes, sir."

I should mention a couple of other things in regard to those radio programs. One important factor in convincing people of the merits of our efforts was the fact that we were actually a very conservative group, because our aim was to uphold the letter of the Constitution. We wanted to preserve its meaning, and in a sense we were aiming at what might be called a "strict construction" interpretation of the Constitution. This stand apparently had a great deal of influence on the listeners. I was also frankly astonished at the extent to which the phone calls reflected a predominant, if not overwhelming, public agreement with the Bill and against the war.

Now this is not to say that there were not people in opposition; I've already mentioned one case. But I would say that the heavy majority of people were not initially antagonistic and they remained favorable, judging by their phone calls.

Turning now to the day of the testimony, my overall impression is that the session was handled beautifully by Shea, Wells, and Worth. They had done a marvelous job of advance arrangements. There were, as you will no doubt find out in other portions of this book, so many people at the hearing that it had to be moved to a larger auditorium. The room was filled with people from every age group: young, old, and middle-aged. I have been told that this in itself was very impressive to the Judiciary Committee. Jim Shea made a good introduction; Tigar was excellent; and Warren Schwartz, who has many more reservations about the legal aspects of the Bill than perhaps I do, nevertheless gave a very effective presentation. I must add that Wells was fine, and Worth was his usual brilliant, oratorical self.

It was really overwhelming to see the number of people in the audience who responded wholeheartedly and spontaneously. Some of them, of course had come as representatives of organizations with the specific purpose of speaking up, but there were others who had apparently just come there to listen and ended up popping up and talking. The way the testimony was handled in the Massachusetts legislature was one of the finest contributions to democracy I had ever seen; I mean the fact that the session was open-ended, which meant that anybody who wanted to could just get up and testify before the legislature. Clearly it is a system that can be abused if too many people were to take too much time testifying. I suspect that sort of thing doesn't happen or else the rule for open-ended testimony would have been changed a long time ago. But on this occasion it was fantastic to see young and old people, all kinds of people, getting up to state their views.

That night there was a party at John's house in Lexington, and I had a delightful time among people with whom I felt a complete *rapport*. After the party Jim Shea took me back to my hotel and he and his aide, Businger, and another fellow named Rosenblith came up to my room. We sat there for several hours, drinking the dark beer Shea loved, and talking.

The next day I flew home but I kept in touch often with Steve, John, and Bob Condlin, talking about what progress the Bill was making, what had to be done, and so forth. I should say a few words about Bob at this point. After I gave my testimony and was listening to somebody else, a young fellow came up to me and shook my hand and said that he always wanted to meet me because in preparing his court brief on the legality of the war a year or two ago, he had relied heavily on an article of mine. Since that day, Bob and I have been in continuous contact especially on procedures. I list this encounter, as well as the friendships I made with other people in Boston, as one of the boons of having been there.

Just before the Bill came to a vote, Steve called me to ask for my help in a telegram campaign. I managed to round up about a dozen professors around the country to send wires urging the Bill be passed. The telegrams Steve and I obtained were apparently of some consequence in knocking down one of the main arguments that was being made against the Bill, namely that it was illegal.

Our association kept up in other ways. When Andrew Stein brought up a similar Bill in New York and wanted people to testify in New York City in behalf of his Bill, John, Steve, and I were glad to help out. We saw each other in Illinois, too, where we all testified in behalf of a Bill introduced by Bob Mann of the Illinois legislature.

These men and the Massachusetts people who worked with them deserve the thanks of the entire nation. They rekindled the war issue when it should have been rekindled, when the Administration had succeeded in having it die down, and they gave hope to the people of Massachusetts. Since then similar bills have been brought up in other states. I think that the nation owes a great deal of thanks to these people and that they deserve a lot more than a mere footnote in a history book.

8 "My Name Is Dr. Robin Alison Remington"

Robin Remington

My name is Dr. Robin Alison Remington. I am a Research Associate at the M.I.T. Center for International Studies. I do not represent any organization. I am speaking for myself. I want to speak as a witness in support of House Bill 2396 because this is the first time in five years that I have not been ashamed to be an American.

The Chairman of the Judiciary Committee, Sen. Joseph Ward started slightly. We looked at each other. I knew how deeply what I said was true. I knew how badly I had wanted to say it—that that was why, after almost five hours of public hearing my feet had somehow brought me from a far corner of the balcony to the front rows. For I had not planned to speak at all; nor am I sure if this is exactly what I said, because the Judiciary Committee kept no records. It does not matter. The substance is the same, if not the language.

The words almost seemed to say themselves. I come from a New England family with a long tradition of public service; a tradition that can survive only while there are channels through which a people can affect the operation of their government. And on the issue of war and peace the government in Washington has become increasingly deaf. . . . I thought of November, 1969; of Richard Nixon's contemptuous refusal to listen to any but the silent voices in which he heard an echo of his own rhetoric. I consider this war a disaster on both human and professional grounds.

69

For, ever since we started bombing North Vietnam, on February 8, 1965, this country has been more and more trapped by its unwillingness to admit mistakes. Even accepting the premise that communism as an ideology threatens our global interests, Vietnam is the wrong war, at the wrong time, with the wrong enemy. It is a response to the cold war paranoia of the 1950's, an attempt incorrectly to treat the Communist world as a monolithic force just as that world is most divided, to apply the containment policy developed for Soviet communism in Europe to Asia where historical and political realities are different. There is an intrinsic absurdity in the idea of fighting China by bombing North Vietnam or even by rooting out the Vietcong in the South. That absurdity has a high price—forty-two thousand American soldiers dead, $30 billion a year objectively spent in destroying the country we would save, savage splits in the fabric of our own society, and a growing isolation of our government from the American people.

Quite apart from the immorality of inflicting that kind of punishment on any people to serve our own interests, the Vietnam war has been a political liability. It has made our embassies around the world constant objects of attack and has damaged relations with the Soviet Union at a time when there are far more important things involved in those relations than the issues at stake in Vietnam.

But today I am more interested in the domestic implications. For this war has upset the traditional system of checks and balances even as it severed the links of trust necessary between a people and those who govern. Congress has become a shadow, offering token objections to a President who considers advice and consent to mean acquiescence after the fact. This hearing is important because it offers hope that on some level of government people can be heard. This law is important because it is a desperate, half-chance to correct the process without destroying it.

After I had spoken, Senator Ward leaned forward: "Do you feel better about the possibility of this system's working now?" It was an honest question—neither as trite nor as patronizing as it looks written down.

I felt the anger of five years' outrage; outrage against a President who would violate my humanity by fighting this obscene war in the name of "American Honor," lie to Congress to get the Gulf of Tonkin Resolution, and then resign because he could not cope with the ills he had created; outrage at Richard Nixon's "secret way" to end the war in Vietnam even as he quietly escalated American bombing in Laos, turning one quarter of that country's population into political refugees living in uninhabitable camps to carry out the Pentagon's theory that the Pathet Lao will find it hard to fight a people's war with fewer and fewer people.

I answered: "Only if you act. The right to dissent without influence is nothing. If this committee listens to this hearing and then prevents the Bill from coming to the floor of the legislature, it will have been a useless exercise."

We looked at each other again. Senator Ward spoke slowly: "The measure of this system is its ability to change. We do not have to have a revolution to change here, but change is not always rapid. The test is not in whether any one issue succeeds."

I had started to go to my seat but turned back for a final word: "The test is exactly whether or not a system can be made to work. I study revolution in my profession and that study shows that historically when processes do not work, when governments do not follow their own rules, they fall. There comes a time when a people no longer believes that tomorrow will be better than yesterday and cannot endure." Sitting down I thought, that time is now. Two Presidents have usurped the powers of Congress, burdening us with an illegal, immoral executive war. Mayor Daley's police brutalized Eugene McCarthy's supporters during the 1968 Democratic National Convention. His totalitarian response was furthered by Judge Hoffman's mockery of justice during the "Conspiracy" trial of the Chicago seven, some of whom had never met each other prior to their arrest. The army keeps computer-data banks of intelligence information about the political beliefs and activities of anti-war demonstrators.

Small wonder that students write on walls, occupy offices, and break windows. When there is no respect for "law and order" at the highest level of government, disorder below can be expected. Indeed the response is not so different. When Mr. Nixon is frustrated by his impotence to control the political life of Indochina by fiat from Washington, he invades Cambodia. There was no checking on public opinion before the fact. There was no prior consultation with Congress. There is even evidence that much of the State Department was caught flatfooted; that the normal procedure of in-depth analyses of possible Soviet, Chinese, and North Vietnamese reactions was abandoned. That is flagrant abuse of presidential authority. In such a context it is not surprising that when anti-war protesters are frustrated by trying to talk to a President who has plainly said he will not listen, more extreme elements of the April 15 Moratorium riot in Harvard Square. Only Mr. Nixon is more dangerous—the demonstrators trashed an area of a few blocks in their frustration; he has the power to trash whole countries, committing American men and money to endless presidential wars. It is a frightening prospect.

It does not matter that Cambodia had not happened yet. The pattern was clear, and like any rational person I was afraid. That is a good part of why I came to work with the diffuse yet intensely close group of people that made the Shea Bill move from an idea in Rev. John Wells's head into Massachusetts law. When John asked me to describe that process to help fill in the picture of how we came together as a group, I felt a loose, awkward hesitation. I am no stranger to political analysis. But there is a world of difference in *ex post facto* explanation of what happened and knowing what turns someone on to a particular issue. Perhaps especially so when that someone is yourself. For political behavior has deep roots in who you are, which makes for problems of objectivity as readers of Norman Mailer's account of the 1967 March on the Pentagon know. Unfortunately for this task, I am not Norman Mailer.

Professionally I am Dr. Remington, a Research Associate in Communist Studies at the Massachusetts Institute of Technology's Center for International Studies and a Lecturer in the M.I.T. Humanities Department. My own research is primarily in Soviet East European politics. Last year I edited a documentary on the 1968 attempt to sweep the ashes of Stalinism from the Czechoslovakian road to socialism. Next year I will be in Belgrade studying Yugoslavian attitudes toward European security.

On a day-by-day basis I help organize what is probably the largest unclassified, publicly available documentation center on communism, revisionism, and revolution in the United States. This aspect of my work is the most relevant, for when one follows the problems of Communist pluralism in a detailed way and sees the increasing predominance of domestic-nationalist considerations in Communist parties and states throughout the world, the Johnson-Nixon policy statements on United States involvement in Vietnam take on a stark obsolescence. They are responding to a world that is not there; that perhaps never was. That response has all the properties of a self-ful- filling prophecy. For the domino theory has as much reality as our actions give it. Sihanouk was basically neutral. By supporting his rivals and invading Cambodia, we have guaranteed that he could return only in the arms of the Chinese. North Vietnam has fought to remain independent from both Moscow and Peking; yet the punishing war against the United States and South Vietnamese forces Hanoi to rely more and more heavily on these two Communist giants for military aid. Moreover, we are rapidly undermining the delicate balance that has existed in Laos since 1962. Even if American troops leave Indochina, we will have effectively destroyed any moderate forces, eliminating the middle from the political spectrum so that these hapless peoples will have only the choice of a left or right dictatorship. It is not a pretty choice.

But where I have arrived politically is not a professional decision; rather my profession is important because it gives me access to facts. I object to the Vietnam war as an American citizen whose national honor has been abused, whose sense of social well-being has been shattered, whose money is misused, and whose brothers are endangered by a senseless and fundamentally illegal battle to prop up a corrupt dictatorship. I object to it as an infringement on my daily life, replacing the happier moments of my nonworking world when I would prefer to study *batik* or dance, with an unending political priority. Perhaps most of all I object to that war as un-American; as an Orwellian violation of all that this country stands for when it stands for anything at all. And here who I am becomes more complicated, because, although I am not a Republican, my political identification goes back through many generations of bedrock New England Republicans dedicated to an image of public service. They were a people to whom John Quincy Adams was not only history but a way of life. I was brought up on his speeches; accepting that

> Wherever the standard of freedom and independence has been or shall be unfurled there will be America's heart, her benedictions, and her prayers. But she goes not abroad in search of monsters to destroy.... She well knows that by enlisting under other banners than her own, were they even the banners of foreign independence, she would involve herself beyond the power of extrication, in all wars of interest and intrigue, of individual avarice, envy and ambition, which assume the colors and usurp the standards of freedom. The fundamental maxims of her policy would insensibly change from liberty to force ... she might become dictatress of the world. She would no longer be the ruler of her own spirit.
>
> (July 4, 1821)

Shaken by the depression and still more scattered during World War II, the family divided when I was young. I went with my mother and stepfather to Texas. The South has a way of educating outsiders. In Texas I learned what it meant to be an alien, part of an isolated minority of damnyankees. Ours was a community that refused to have its children socialized to the value that a man's worth is in the color of his skin, his physical strength, or his power to buy the law. (That is not to say there were not Southerners who felt the same—only that as a child I never met them.) We were taught the Constitution as a living document above state or even national law. Indeed one of my earliest political memories is of family discussions on the unconstitutional nature of an accumulative, selectively applied poll tax.

When my stepfather died, we could not afford to return North. Living two steps on the right side of want, I learned to hate the hypocrisy that condemned the fathers of my Latino friends as shiftless for not working while barring them from unions and tolerating a standard of welfare that could be considered livable only when Mexican children ate from garbage cans in the early mornings. Prevailing opinion can be a deceptive measure of right or wrong.

But I was white and had the advantage of a family that had known another world. Mother, who used books to escape much of the daily unpleasantness, had taught me to think of an education as a realistic alternative to the perpetual backache of earning twenty-five dollars a week at Woolworth's. So—after being turned down by the WAC (which I had tried to join during a fit of depression at ever finding work) for being undersize—I went to Southwest Texas State College with whatever I had earned at odd jobs and a promise of seventy-five cents an hour working for the college news service. The news-service job expanded into one as a reporter on the San Marcos weekly. That led to summers on the Galveston *Daily News* where I came to know more than was comfortable about the unchecked brutality of a police department that considered itself above the law, and the unlimited ugliness of racial hate. It was a crash course in the mechanics of repression long before we were admitting that underside of the political process. Unlike many Americans who are not quite sure what the charge of political repression means, suspect it of being radical rhetoric, and would like to deny its existence, I have an unambiguous understanding of that issue.

When Mr. Nixon cites the depth of anti-war protest to deny that there is repression of political dissidents, he misses the point. The extent of dissent is not a measure of an unrepressive political system, nor is the low visibility of armed force during the May 10 anti-war rally in Washington. Rather, political repression means much more than what happens in Mr. Nixon's backyard. It speaks to the systematic misuse of their monopoly of legal violence by local and national authorities.

When the National Guard fires into a crowd of protesting students without warning; when New York police allow a mob of construction workers to attack demonstrators; when off-duty policemen can beat members of the Black Panther Party in a courtroom with impunity, that is repression.

I was nineteen years old when a deputy sheriff threatened to run me out of Galveston County for writing a news story that he did not like. I was lucky. I knew that one year before while the former sheriff, who treated the county as his private fiefdom for twenty years, was still in office, I could have been found dead like the young man in the offending article. I knew that ordinary people (white and black) would rather take their chances in a back alley than with the local police. That is repression.

The next year I left Texas with a research assistantship to study international law and politics at Indiana University. I left with the firm conviction that the object of study is not only to understand the world but to change it.

It was a conviction that went with me from Indiana back to Massachusetts when I returned East to write my dissertation at the Harvard Russian Research Center. It was that conviction that prodded me to the State House for the public hearing on House Bill 2396.

I didn't much want to go. February 11, 1970 was a grey, cold day. I was still struggling with the aftermath of Asian flu and suppressing a sour memory of being inadvertently gassed during the November Moratorium in Washington. Thinking that at least the State House would be warmer than the Boston Common, I took the subway to Park Street. After all, it was not every day one had a chance to sit down and be counted.

Some eight hundred people crowded into the hearing room; as many more were turned away. Typical of much political action, it began late. A rather flustered man apologized for the delay. The Judiciary Committee had bogged down on an earlier hearing. They had not expected so many people—neither had any of us. We waited.

The Committee appeared at 2 o'clock. Senator Ward looked out across the waiting faces. He congratulated the number of young people on their interest in the issues; then said quietly: "This committee is impressed by facts, and by reasoned argument. It is not impressed by emotional display. If there are outbursts, I will be forced to end the hearing and we will all have to come back another day." The line was drawn. You could almost hear your neighbor trying to breathe less loudly. It had been elegantly done. I decided that I liked Joe Ward's style even though I knew nothing of his opinions and said a silent prayer that there were not any guerrilla-theater advocates in the crowd.

The hearing began. It was one of those fragile collective happenings that resist words. Representative Jim Shea introduced the bill. Reverend John Wells spoke (in his fantastic Georgia accent) of his inability to live in the house of Jonathan Harrington on Lexington Green and not seek a solution. Former Alaskan Senator Gruening attacked "the conspiracy at the highest level of government to hornswoggle the elected representatives of the people" to ensure passage of the Gulf of Tonkin Resolution. I felt as if I had fallen forward into an ongoing American revolution. Perhaps the magic of that hearing was hope. For the first time since 1965 when we sloshed into Montgomery, Alabama, ending the Selma-Montgomery march with a demonstration that had even President Johnson saying "we shall overcome," I was politically happy.

When Senator Ward asked for the sense of the audience three hours later and only one hand was raised in opposition to the Bill, I almost forgot to breathe. The constitutional issue cut into conflicting constituencies. Not only could it depend on the anti-war support, but it could pick up conservatives who feared the unprecedented growth of presidential power, and it might even reach those who favored the war but wanted it fought by a united nation. Surely at least a smattering of hard-core hawks should favor a court case. Even if we lost, the Bill had enormous possibilities for educational work among communities more overtly militant protests leave untouched.

And there was more than a chance that we just might win. I could feel the inner excitement like a drug. The deeply intuitive sense of rightness was so strong that I never realized exactly when I had begun thinking "we." The next morning I called Jim Shea and asked what needed to be done. Jim said come to a meeting in Lexington. I had dealt myself in.

From that moment until April 2, 1970 when Governor Sargent signed the Bill into law, I lived the Shea-Wells Bill as the best going channel for resistance to an illegitimate authority. For despite the current myth that only the President has the information necessary to make decisions of war and peace, the White House comes equipped with a hotline to Moscow not God. We all pay the price and share the guilt for the atrocity of Vietnam.

The rest is recent history. How did it happen? None of us really know. Oh, we could diagram the organization—a flexible, fluctuating center with heavy responsibility at the edges. The non-exclusiveness was crucial; it was a multipurpose issue and everyone was welcome. You did what you saw was needed and touched base later.

The Bill moved because it was the right time. It moved because all the pieces came together—Jim Shea, John Wells, Steve Worth; Rep. Cornelius Kiernan, House Speaker David Bartley, Sen. Joseph Ward; Jean Rostoker, who organized the Fitchburg rally single-handed; Lee Goldstein, the Saugus High School students, and countless others. It moved because it was a respectable way for a sizeable slice of the silent majority to say we have had enough. It moved because participation became reality instead of myth and large numbers of ordinary people put aside the reality of apathy and worked like hell.

We were a government of, by, and for the people-now lobby. Or in the current shorthand—power to the people.

For no president should be able to commit American blood and treasure to foreign wars without even the pretext of national debate. It is not consulting Congress or informing the public to release the figures of how many pilots die over Laos without discussing why those men (and the Laotians they bomb) should die.

Now Jim Shea is dead and should be counted among the casualties of Mr. Nixon's Cambodian adventure. For despite his surface optimism Jim must have felt more deeply than any of us the despair of going two steps back; the impotence of a victory that moved too slowly to halt a seemingly endlessly expanding war. We don't know. And in a quiet part of myself I refuse to admit that he is gone.

9

The Betrayal at Tonkin Gulf

Senator Ernest Gruening

When I was asked to speak for the Shea-Wells Bill, I felt it was a privilege and an honor to be asked to appear before the General Court in Massachusetts, particularly on an issue of such transcendental and historic importance.

This issue, embodied in House Bill 2936, is to provide that no citizen of Massachusetts shall be compelled to serve in the Armed Services of the United States in an undeclared war.

The purpose of this legislation is to test whether the war in Vietnam in which the United States has been engaged for some five years at the cost of much blood and treasure is not in violation of Article I, Section 8 of the Constitution, which provides that only the Congress of the United States can declare war. The Congress has made no such declaration. Nevertheless, as a result of actions by the executive branch of the government we have been plunged into a costly war in Southeast Asia, which in my view and in the view of an ever-increasing number of Americans, was wholly needless, unjustified, immoral, and monstrous.

It is highly fitting that this legislation, originated ideologically by Massachusetts citizens such as the Reverend John Wells, Pastor of the Unitarian Universalist Church of Lexington, and others, should first be proposed among the many states by the State of Massachusetts. This is in accord with the great libertarian traditions of this great state, a state that has always been in the forefront of every one of our nation's unceasing battles for freedom.

It was here that the embattled farmers stood and fired the shot heard around the world.

It was here that Concord and Lexington were followed by Bunker Hill.

It was here in Boston that Crispus Attucks shed the first blood in our struggle for independence.

It is here that Fanueil Hall commemorates those early struggles for liberty.

It was here in William Lloyd Garrison's garret that "the freedom of a race began."

What the Legislature of Massachusetts is initiating today is a continuation and reaffirmation of the historic leadership of Massachusetts in freedom's cause.

Apart from the undeniable merit of that cause and my gratitude for being permitted to play a very minor part in it, I have a personal attachment and bonds to the Bay State.

I received my higher education across the Charles River in our nation's oldest institution of higher learning. My wife was born here in Boston. It was in Massachusetts that I courted her, here that we were married, and here that we honeymooned. My three sons were all born in Massachusetts.

So I was more than proud to come back to Massachusetts and tender what aid I could to this great and worthy objective.

It is all that and more. For the military involvement of the United States half way around the world in the jungles of Southeast Asia constitutes, in my view, the most tragic and costly mistake made by our country in its long and generally glorious history. Indeed, it is a betrayal of our long-honored principles and professions. Unlike earlier wars, such as World War II when the United States was wantonly attacked at Pearl Harbor, we were not, in this war, attacked; no vital interest of the United States was in jeopardy. Indeed, we barged half way around the world to inject ourselves into a civil war that we had a large part in precipitating.

In doing so we violated all of our treaties to which our nation is a signatory, the United Nations Charter which we had the major part in devising, the SEATO Treaty and the agreement to abide by the Geneva Accords and permit free elections of all Vietnam. And treaties, according to the Constitution, are the highest law of the land.

Our people were misled into this war. The official reasons given in justification for our being there are without foundation.

It is not true, as Lyndon Baines Johnson asserted in his first State of the Union Message, that we are there because a friendly government asked us to come in and help it to repel aggression. The record is wholly bare of any such request. On the contrary, we asked ourselves in. And when we landed our troops and began bombing that small country of Vietnam—North and South—it is, I regret to state, the United States that became the aggressor. In the course of this aggression we have permitted crimes of the kind which we unsparingly and properly denounced decades earlier when committed by the totalitarian rulers of Nazi Germany, Fascist Italy and Communist Russia.

When President Johnson several months after his State of the Union misrepresentation repeated it in his Johns Hopkins address saying that three Presidents had pledged that military support, he was again falsifying history. President Eisenhower never offered military aid; he proferred only economic aid and that surrounded by conditions that were never fulfilled. President Kennedy sent military advisors—mistakenly, it is now clear—but the first President to send our troops into combat was Lyndon Baines Johnson, and he did this in violation of his repeated pledges made during his presidential election campaign of 1964 that he would not send our boys to fight a ground war on the continent of Asia; that he would not send American boys to do the fighting that Asian boys should be doing.

And while he was making these solemn promises on the basis of which he was swept into office, the Pentagon was maturing plans—and of course with his knowledge—to do the very things he had promised the American people he would not do.

Then in August of 1964 came the so-called Tonkin Gulf incident. In a message drafted in the White House and sent to the Congress requesting speedy action, the President alleged that an American destroyer peaceably cruising on a routine patrol mission in International waters had been wantonly attacked by North Vietnamese PT boats, and he asked the Congress in consequence to give him authority to use the armed forces of the United States as he saw fit anywhere in Southeast Asia.

The Congress, of course, did not know that this presentation of what had happened was wholly false. As revealed in hearings before the Senate Committee on Foreign Relations several years later, it developed that the destroyer in question, the *Maddox*, was not on a routine patrol in International waters. She was first of all a spy ship like the *Pueblo* and equipped with all the electronic equipment for such a ship. Second, she was not in International waters; she had penetrated the coastal waters of North Vietnam. And third, she was doing it at the very time a raid by South Vietnamese vessels supplied by the United States and directed by our Navy were engaging in an attack on North Vietnamese ports, an attack in which the *Maddox* was asked to participate to the extent of trying to draw away some of the North Vietnamese vessels from that engagement. So the North Vietnamese were fully justified in considering the *Maddox* engaged in a hostile operation and firing upon her. Nevertheless none of the shots hit her. The further statement from the White House that on the next day there was another attack on an American destroyer, the *C. Turner Joy,* was likewise unfounded.

In this deception all of our highest officials participated: the President of the United States, Lyndon Baines Johnson, the Secretary of State Dean Rusk, the Secretary of Defense Robert McNamara, the brothers Bundy, the brothers Rostow, and the High Naval Command in the Pacific.

And so the United States was lied into this war with the consequences that there are now forty thousand fine young American boys dead, three hundred thousand wounded, some of them crippled for life, blinded, armless, legless, paralyzed; tens of thousands of noncombatants—old men, women and children in both North and South Vietnam, the latter being the country we are allegedly there to save—slaughtered; millions made homeless refugees, and all of the other disastrous consequences of our leaderships's folly.

These consequences include the betrayal of our most cherished traditions and the consequent loss of respect and affection for us throughout most of the so-called free world: the irrecoverable loss of $125 billion sunk into the Asian quagmire, while our long overdue domestic needs—education, housing, pollution abatement, slum clearance, crime control, and much else—go unattended; the alienation of our young people who have lost faith in our system which those of us of an older generation have always admired and cherished and wish to love and cherish again.

One may say also, as a capstone of our folly, that if the rulers of Communist Russia and Communist China who undoubtedly do not wish us well, had wanted to devise a policy that would bring our nation down they could not have invented one more designed to bring about that result than the one the United States has been pursuing under the misleadership of its executive branch.

That, apart from the vital principle and abstract values involved, would be ample justification for the attempt of Massachusetts to restore the power to make war where it belongs—in the representative body elected by the people of the United States—the Congress.

10   Grass Roots Political Action

I. John Dixon Elder

Citizens for Participation Politics, the outgrowth of the Eugene McCarthy campaign in Massachusetts, drafted its first platform in a convention held on the campus of Holy Cross College in Worcester, Massachusetts, on Sunday, May 11, 1969. The platform planks were drafted in workshop sessions, and among the planks drafted by the workshop on "Militarization and Foreign Policy" was the following: "Resolved that the power to declare war be restored to the Congress of the United States, and that no American troops be committed to any military action without a specific declaration of war."

The workshop was chaired by Prof. Edgar Bottome of Boston University, but I am unable to determine who actually drafted the plank. The plank did not receive a unanimous vote at the convention, and therefore it was submitted to delegates and local groups for their vote. Exception to the plank was taken by Michael McGonnigal of Weymouth, who argued, "I believe that there are situations in which the President must act without the consent of Congress. In such cases, the members of Congress as a whole, within five days, must order a continuance of a cessation of the action or vote for a continuance of the debate." Thus there was no substantial disagreement with what finally emerged as the Shea Bill, and the plank passed overwhelmingly in the mail ballot by delegates and local groups.

CPP groups devoted a great deal of time and energy to the Vietnam Moratorium during the Summer and Fall, although 6th Congressional District groups concentrated on the congressional campaign of Michael Harrington against Saltonstall. The success of that campaign in the special general election on September 30 was widely interpreted as evidence of the strong "peace vote" in Massachusetts, and the credit Harrington gave to CPP for its role greatly added to CPP prestige state-wide.

My personal contact with the Rev. John Wells began when I became Acting Director of Field Education at Harvard Divinity School. The First Parish of Lexington requested a team of students to serve the church through the field-education program of Harvard. Four students were placed with First Parish under the supervision of Mr. Wells and the Assistant Minister, Mrs. Barbara Holleroth. I had several conversations with Mr. Wells during September and October, primarily in relation to the plans for a Vietnam Moratorium rally on the Lexington Green, though also concerning the field-education project. The Lexington CPP group worked actively on the Moratorium, as well as the November 15 Moratorium in Washington.

In early December Mr. Wells phoned me to explain that he was drafting a Bill to preserve the constitutional rights of G.I.'s not to be forced to fight overseas in undeclared wars. He wanted to know my reaction and also whether CPP would support such legislation. I agreed with him that although passage of the Bill seemed to be impossible, it would be valuable to file the legislation to try to raise the question of the constitutionality of the war and force as much debate as possible on the issue.

The bi-weekly CPP *Coordinator Bulletin* is sent to some 400 political activists in the 130 communities in Massachusetts with CPP groups. The first notice of the Shea Bill is in *Coordinator Bulletin No. 23* (February 6, 1970), which states:

> Another, even more immediate, focus of antiwar activity is the Wells Bill (H. 2396). This proposed legislation would prevent the sending of any Massachusetts citizen to Vietnam unless there is a congressional declaration of war. It promises to raise decisively the issue of the constitutionality of the war and the absorption of power by the Executive branch. The hearing on this important Bill is next Wednesday, February 11 (the unusually hasty scheduling of the bill by the Judiciary Committee is unfortunate and perhaps not unintentional). Among those testifying for

the Bill will be former Sen. Ernest Gruening. Similar legislation has been introduced in the U.S. House and in other states.

A copy of the Bill was enclosed with the *Bulletin.*

Previous to this notice in the *Coordinator Bulletin,* CPP local groups were being alerted by phone of the need to have as many people as possible at the hearing. The intense telephone campaign continued right up to the hearing, with CPP, PAX, and others supporting the Bill cooperating to turn out as many people as possible.

I was in touch with John Wells throughout December and January, although my concern tended to be more for the congressional contests already beginning to shape up in the 3rd, 10th, and 12th Districts. CPP Headquarters had available on its literature table information on the Bill as soon as it became available. I attended the press conference held by John Wells, Jim Shea, and Steve Worth at the State House (Rm 443) at 11 a.m., Monday, January 26. CPP was alerted to the calling of the conference too late to get many people there, but I noticed that the Harvard Divinity School field-education students were present along with a number of young people from the First Parish. Richard Cauchi, Executive Secretary of CPP, went with me and commented that it was highly unusual to hold a press conference at the State House when a Bill was filed. However, it seemed clear that any means of bringing attention to the Bill would be justified, since it had no chance of passing and could at best stimulate debate. (I do not recall meeting Jim Shea before the press conference, though he had been a CPP-endorsed candidate in 1968, the only non-incumbent CPP candidate elected.)

The first critical point in the campaign for the Shea-Wells Bill was the hearing before the Judiciary Committee on February 11. We distributed as widely as possible the handbills Fred King produced in record speed, and I would guess that at least half the eight hundred people who packed the Gardner Auditorium had been contacted through CPP (though probably also through other groups in many cases).

I testified briefly on behalf of the Bill as follows:

Members of the Judiciary Committee: The Bill before you this afternoon may well be the most significant item of legislation to be considered by this session of the Great and General Court. The function of this Bill is not to favor any particular group or organization nor to condemn any administration or Congress, but to protect the constitutional rights of all citizens. Those who favor this Bill are not unpatriotic nor disloyal. They seek to restore to Congress the powers and responsibilities granted to it by the United States Constitution. They recognize the truth of what one great President, himself no weak executive in the waging of war, said about the issue with which this legislation deals. I quote Abraham Lincoln:

> "The provision of the Constitution giving the war power to Congress was dictated, as I understand it, by the following reasons; kings had always been involving and impoverishing their people in wars, pretending generally, if not always, that the good of the people was their object. This our Constitution understood to be the most oppressive of all kingly oppressions and they resolved to so frame the Constitution that no one man should hold the power of bringing this oppression upon us."

> House 2396 embodies a resolution voted by Citizens for Participation Politics, a state-wide organization of some 130 local groups with approximately 3,000 members, at its platform convention held on May 11, 1969. Although it was submitted by Rep. James Shea on petition of Rev. John M. Wells, it represents the concern and conviction of thousands of Massachusetts citizens that due process of government must be restored. At a time when "law and order" is of such national interest, what could be more important than respect for the nation's highest law and conformity to the governmental order established by our founding fathers? House 2396 is an important step toward both the renewal of law and order in the highest meaning of that phrase and the restoration of a nation suffering for far too many years—and at the expense of far too many lives—in "the President's War."

> On behalf of Citizens for Participation Politics, I urge your favorable recommendation of this legislation.

The hearing had begun with a humorous incident. Fred King's little daughter ran up in front of the long table behind which the members of the Senate Judiciary Committee were seated and made the peace sign. Sen. Joseph Ward, Chairman of the Committee, had the wit to respond with a smile and a peace sign, but he warned against outbursts of emotion and demonstrations. All the testimony was extremely impressive; but I personally felt that Prof. Steve Worth was most persuasive, since he carefully argued precisely those points that members of the Committee were most likely to be concerned about. At the end of my own testimony Sen. Phil Pellegrini of Arlington, my own senator, leaned over and said, "That was very sincere"—which gave me no clue as to how he was likely to vote.

During the next four weeks CPP worked actively to lobby with members of the Judiciary Committee. The *Coordinator Bulletin* of February 21 listed the members of the Committee and their phone numbers. The *Bulletin* of March 6 predicted a favorable report from the Committee and urged members to shift their attention to lobbying with state representatives, and to attend the House sessions during which the Bill was debated. CPP pressure was clearly instrumental in changing some votes. I talked with my representative, Gregory Khachadoorian, who changed his vote, and phoned Michael Harrington to ask him to try to influence his successor. The galleries were packed, and many of the people present were CPP members, who were also organizing telephone and telegram campaigns.

The *Coordinator Bulletin* of March 20 reports the passage of the Shea-Wells Bill by the House and urges pressure on the Senate and the governor. It includes a paragraph of arguments to use in lobbying, and a listing of the roll-call vote. In the *Coordinator Bulletin* of April 3, CPP members were urged to wire Governor Sargent asking him to sign the Bill.

The victory celebration at Larry Adler's in Lexington on April 3 was a happy event indeed. Many of the people there were CPP members, and it was evident that CPP could indeed take some credit for the miracle legislative act of the year, though obviously the creative force was the Wells-Shea-Worth triumvirate.

II. Richard Cauchi

The year 1968 was a most significant one in the history of political development and ideas in the state of Massachusetts. For out of the mass movement known as the McCarthy campaign came the beginnings of a new concept in state and local politics. Labeled "New Politics" or "Citizen Politics," it embodied the idea that issues and direct citizen involvement were more important than party names or the personality cults of the more traditional style of politics in this state.

It took almost a full year for the former McCarthy workers in the divergent cities and towns of the Bay State to set aside their bitterness at the system and decide on a firm direction for their future political activity. The guidelines for that future action were spelled out at a state-wide convention of the organization that emerged as the major force of new politics: Citizens for Participation Politics.

The "Militarization and Foreign Policy Committee," which emerged as a permanent body authorized to take action on approved platform items, soon became involved in plans and publicity for the newly conceived Vietnam Moratorium, in cooperation with Jerome Grossman of Mass. PAX and Sam Brown (formerly of Cambridge). No action was taken by CPP on the resolution about unauthorized wars because the members, who were not constitutional lawyers, had not even thought action was possible on a state legislative level. Instead CPP and the other advocates of peace and new politics turned to more direct electoral activity in the form of support for State Rep. Michael Harrington, who had been persuaded to run for Congress in a special election held in the Summer of 1969. Mr. Harrington's success in that Democratic primary and then in the main election against a pro-Nixon hawk (State Sen. William Saltonstall) did much to show that there was a strong and unified peace effort in Massachusetts, which could be directed into real, localized, political campaigns.

However, while the members of CPP worked on the Moratorium, and contemplated how to best utilize the powers and talents of Congressman Harrington (an early McCarthy supporter and CPP member), Rev. John Wells independently conceived a means of drafting the concept of "protecting the rights of servicemen in undeclared wars" into workable legislation on the state level. The "new politics" forces played no real role until mid-December, when associates of State Rep. H. James Shea, Jr. (who had been endorsed by CPP in the Fall of 1968 during his first try for the state legislature) mentioned that such a Bill had indeed been written and filed.

During the early weeks of January, I attended several informational discussions about the prospects of this Bill at Jim Shea's State House office at the invitation of John Businger, a fellow CPP member and former associate from the days when we both worked in College Young Democrats. Since I had been coordinating the CPP citizens lobby effort at the Massachusetts State House during the previous session, I was at first interested more in the practical effects of this Bill than in the broader constitutional implications.

At these January meetings few of us thought the Bill had any real chance of passage; however, I was enthusiastic about the attempt for several reasons. First, it would provide an effective public forum for expression of anti-war sentiment, both by average citizens and legal experts. Second, it would force the 280 members of the legislature officially to notice the entire issue, and hopefully, express their opinions by means of a roll-call vote. Third, it was a good opportunity to pressure other public officials such as mayors, city councillors, selectmen, etc., to take a position, since anything in the form of official legislation had a certain air of legitimacy and respectability. In addition, it was a very good means of renewing activism "in the movement," since more conventional peace-oriented projects seemed to stagnate during the winter months. Finally, a few of us hoped it could show that the State Legislature was indeed a significant political force, worth the attention of many more concerned citizens.

Following a meeting with Representative Shea, Professor Worth and Reverend Wells on January 22, the CPP members most familiar with procedures at the State House began making plans for the public hearing which would be held by the Judiciary Committee of the Legislature. Despite difficulties in determining the date such a hearing would be held, CPP immediately concentrated its efforts on spreading the work among the many state-wide and community groups. In addition to the 130 local chapters of CPP, at least 150 organizations were contacted with explanations of the Bill, and urged to attend the hearing, and particularly to testify on behalf of their membership. Throughout this period we sought to have a balanced audience including students, housewives, lawyers, the elderly, and persons from every area of the state. Much of the publicity was spontaneous, as local residents printed their own flyers, brought up the subject at community meetings and Sunday church gatherings, while students made posters and placards. Although there was no budget, nor even a well-defined steering committee, the word did spread rapidly in the few days before the scheduled hearing. The most significant factor, however, was the personal activity of Fred King, a friend of Jim Shea, and a Newton member of CPP. As soon as Fred saw the need for massive leaflets, he went directly to a local sympathetic printer and put forward his own funds to pay for more than twenty thousand flyers announcing the hearing. In any case, the result was that more than one thousand citizens showed up that morning, forcing the Judiciary Committee to move to the largest auditorium in the State House, which still was filled to overflow capacity.

While Reverend Wells and Professor Worth concentrated on lining up nationally known constitutional law experts to testify at the hearing and began efforts to get press coverage on a national scale, some of the CPP members and others who had worked at the State House began to try to line up votes. The only guideline we had to go by was a 1969 roll call on a resolution to prohibit the construction of anti-ballistic missiles (ABMs) anywhere in Massachusetts. This resolution, which had been sponsored by Senate Pres. Maurice Donahue, actually passed the House and Senate. It was the first indication that the State Legislature was willing to act on matters relating to national defense policy. As we talked to the known liberals informally before the hearing, it became clear that those with a legal background were very hesitiant to become embroiled in such a controversial matter at the start of an election year.

III. Jane Webb

Jim Shea was no ordinary man. But in the early months of 1970 these were no ordinary times. Faced with a war in Asia that had dragged on for six years, citizens were discouraged and angry that no accomplishment had resulted. As a freshman legislator in the Massachusetts General Court, Representative Shea had chosen a course to introduce a Bill, by a petitioner Rev. John Wells, that no seasoned politician would have foreseen as a vehicle for either legislative success or personal prestige, much less a rallying point for renewed opposition to the war.

Frustration, disillusion, and despair pervaded the peace movement following the largest national demonstrations on October 15. A feeling of powerlessness gripped those who had tried to change America's policies on Vietnam through public demonstrations, mass rallies, petition drives, and community activities. People had gone to Washington by the hundreds of thousands, had held vigils at the Pentagon, had worked through political parties and still, nothing had really changed.

Massachusetts has been the crucible for much of the anti-war activity in the nation. The idea of a national strike for October 15 was first conceived here at an executive assembly meeting in April, 1969 of Massachusetts Political Action for Peace (PAX). In the early months of 1970, however, after the dust had settled on the rallies, people were asking themselves, "Was our apparent success in October and November really a monumental failure?" The largest protest in history had been blunted by President Nixon's November 3 speech on the Vietnamization of the war and his announcements of minimal troop withdrawal. The peace forces were in disarray, asking themselves where to go from here.

It was in this atmosphere of public disillusion and absence of a new strategy that the idea of testing the constitutionality of the President's power to continue the war without a declaration of Congress became so appealing. The "constitutional question" was indeed a fresh approach that no member of Congress had proposed. And here in Massachusetts a freshman legislator was willing to raise this issue with a Bill in the halls of the Massachusetts General Court.

Up to this point, the Massachusetts peace movement had been more successful in organizing petition drives, letter-writing campaigns, and producing mass demonstrations than in lobbying with legislators or electing candidates. I wondered whether we could be as effective working within the system to pass legislation. The possibility seemed remote in early January, when I first became aware of the Shea Bill. At that time I was Executive Secretary of Massachusetts PAX. Reverend John Wells and John Businger, Representative Shea's legislative assistant, asked for our help. A carefully conceived plan had been mapped out to inform lawyers of this legislation, to gain their support. I was impressed with the long-range, thoughtful advance planning for media coverage that was to precede the hearing of the Bill before the Judiciary Committee on February 11. All the ingredients of a politically sophisticated effort were evident.

I was anxious to provide PAX's help in this initial effort and proposed to our Steering Committee that this Bill might be a major thrust of the anti-war activity in the winter of 1970, to supplant the moribund, dormant strategy of the Moratorium. The Steering Committee agreed to have me write a statement of support for the Bill to the Chairman of the Judiciary Committee, Senator Joseph Ward. I felt organizational statements were important, but not always the crucial factor in legislative success, so I decided to add whatever lobbying expertise I had to the effort.

We began by mailing to our PAX constituents information about the Bill and distributing flyers on the date of the hearing. The response snowballed. People were captivated with the "constitutional" idea of the issue and ran with the ball much in the same way that people in their communities had virtually organized their own activities for October 15. Efforts were largely spontaneous and indigenous rather than highly organized, for the idea caught on at the grass roots level.

No one could have predicted that there would be one of the largest turnouts of citizens in Boston political history at the hearing on February 11 for the Bill at the State House. A skeptical Judiciary Committee listened intently to an auspicious line-up of constitutional lawyers speaking for the Bill, and the Committee's chairman, Sen. Joseph Ward, kept the hearing in session for several hours extending into the dinner hour. For the attendees as well as the legislators, it became a lesson in constitutional history, an enlightened application of constitutional interpretations to the current problems in relation to the war. Could Massachusetts inject itself in a tug-of-war between the powers of the presidency and the powers of the legislative branch? We scurried back to re-read the *Federalist Papers* for renewed insights.

The arguments were appealing. It was hard to oppose an effort to put our constitutional house in order. The continuing tragedy of the war had become an obscenity to many of us who had seen the irrational step-by-step miscalculation of the government's policy. We had seen no ways to brake or reverse the course of American foreign policy into the disastrous quagmire it found itself in Southeast Asia.

I myself had spoken out against the war as early as May 1964, when I stressed the dangers of escalation of our seventeen thousand advisors in Vietnam to a group of five hundred Voice of Women members at the annual meeting in Cambridge.

After six years of frustration the Shea-Wells Bill seemed to me the golden opportunity to channel our hitherto fruitless anti-war efforts into legitimate and effective political action that had not been tried before.

Following the favorable report by the Judiciary Committee, the real work of lobbying began. The first vote in the House on March 16 showed that more than half the legislators were in favor. With two more readings of the Bill required, we made contacts with every member of the House, emphasizing that it was not a diminution of federal power that was implicit in the Bill, but a determination to resolve a crucial constitutional question.

Those of us who helped Jim in this effort grew to know him as someone who worked tirelessly, almost harder than anyone else working with him, yet he was unwilling to take personal credit or power. Modest to the point of being almost self-effacing, Jim soon had working for him a loyal group whose respect and affection grew daily. He developed a team effort in which there was little conflict or criticism; everyone was made to feel an enormously important part of reaching a goal. His consistent politeness testified to a simple faith and quality of innocence that made us all surprised at his eloquence and toughness on the floor debate. He would always stick to the issue, never degrading himself to respond to the *ad hominem* arguments and personal attacks that became more and more abusive. And his persistence and commitment to the issue became a source of great strength for the Bill's ultimate success.

Between the first floor vote and the two following there were several motions for reconsideration. Speaker David Bartley became an important ally, wandering among the representatives' desks urging their support. As for Jim, he worked twenty hours a day, talking to legislators. I myself called legislators directly, and also called many people who I thought would make personal contact with their state representatives. Many of the state representatives later said they had never received so many calls or telegrams from their constituents on any one piece of legislation.

94

Right from the beginning Jim Shea had the vision to stay with a dream and to persuade others that the cause was right. His arguments on the floor in debate on the Bill, running a total of several hours, were concise and brilliant. He fought valiantly with arguments against those who had objections to the Bill. Jim's qualities of courage and leadership in the face of overwhelming odds forged a special kind of loyalty and deep affection among those who worked with him on this legislation. Jim never despaired that the seemingly impossible was insurmountable or unattainable. It was not the charisma of a public leader that drew us to him, but the commitment to a goal and an ideal for which we all cared so much that bound us together in this common effort.

On April 2, when Governor Sargent signed the bill into law, I reflected that here was a young David taking on the Goliath of the government. Perhaps this small step on the part of one State in the Union will begin the process, long overdue, of examining one of the most fundamental constitutional questions that America has faced in its two-hundred-year history. This may be the most exciting contribution of the Shea-Wells Bill. The future will decide.

11   Constructive Dissent

Maurice A. Donahue

When Representative H. James Shea, Jr. testified on February 11, 1970, before the Joint Legislative Committee on the Judiciary in support of his Bill questioning the legality of compelling a citizen of Massachusetts to serve in the military in an undeclared war, he argued that favorable action on his Bill would "again establish Massachusetts as the nation's leader in protecting our constitutional heritage."

Jim Shea was right. And the best memorial to him today is the fact that his Bill has become a national symbol of legitimate and constructive dissent and that Massachusetts, as he predicted, once again has made a notable contribution to the evolution of our (basic) constitutional system.

Jim was appalled, in his words, at the "tragedy of Vietnam," "its serious harm to our international standing," and "its brutalization of our society." But his overriding concern was revealed in his insistence that we should think not just about Vietnam or Cambodia or Laos but about other possible foreign wars: "What about next year's war pursued by an unchecked executive branch without constitutional congressional participation. . . . Continuance of these Executive Wars will inflict limitless harm upon American society."

In essence, Jim Shea was motivated not only by a deep distress at the endless slaughter in Southeast Asia but equally by the fact, as he saw it, that such a war was a direct product of the erosion of the proper balance within our constitutional system between executive authority and legislative responsiblities. He was convinced that, month by month and day by day, we were witnessing "the emergence of an authoritarian executive in the field of foreign affairs" and that the "536-member Congress must be compelled to exercise its full responsibility in the setting of foreign policy."

Representative Shea, by encompassing in his opposition to the current war in Southeast Asia the increasing imbalance within our constitutional system between executive and legislative authority, touched upon an area of concern shared with him by many of his fellow legislators. As much as it is a statement of opposition to the war in Vietnam, the Shea Bill also is a call for a reassertion of responsibility on the part of our national legislature and an end to increasing executive intrusions into areas properly reserved to or shared with other branches of the government. It is an attempt to force consideration of the need for "a reordering of federal power between the legislative and executive branches in accord with the Constitution."

Along with the majority of the members of the Massachusetts General Court, I shared Representative Shea's concern over our tragic involvement in the seemingly endless conflict in Vietnam and with the serious constitutional questions it has raised. On the first Moratorium Day, last October 15, I first raised the possiblity of a prohibition on the use of American draftees overseas in an undeclared war. At that time I noted that, "almost unnoticed, one president after another stretched the elastic limits of presidential power as Commander-in-Chief of the armed forces to commit American men from a limited police action . . . to cover a far more extensive and frustrating involvement in a major land war on the continent of Asia."

At the same time I argued that it is "not sufficient to extricate ourselves from the present quagmire . . . unless we act to avoid similar tragic involvements in the future" and that "we should seriously consider establishing—either through congressional enactment or a formal amendment of the United States Constitution—an absolute prohibition upon the use of draftees or conscripted men for military action outside the United States unless and until there has been a formal declaration of war by the Congress of the United States." I realized that it was necessary that the President should have the ability to respond quickly to threats to our national security or in fulfillment of our obligations abroad, but I thought that necessary power could be retained for the President through the availability of a well-paid, volunteer fighting force which could be employed for police actions or emergencies. In this way, it would still be possible to protect any young man conscripted into military service from being compelled to fight overseas by executive order alone.

The Bill which Representative Shea filed in the Legislature on December 3, 1969, was broader in scope and more specific in detail than my original thoughts had been. His Bill covered all citizens of Massachusetts in military service, whether serving voluntarily or involuntarily, whereas my original thoughts basically concerned draftees ordered into combat overseas. It also required that no citizen of our state could be directed to serve outside the continental United States in an area in which hostilities have been in effect for more than sixty days without a formal congressional declaration of war.

The special and most important feature of Shea's plan was its provision for taking the issue of the war and of the intrusion of executive authority directly to the courts, the branch of the government entrusted by the Constitution to maintain the intended balance of powers and responsibilities in the governing of the nation. In addition, by giving a central role to the attorney general of Massachusetts in providing appeal to the courts, the Shea Bill also gave the state a renewed claim to the importance of its role in serving and protecting the interests of its citizens.

It was this combination of factors—its appeal to those who opposed continuation of the war, its concern with the protection of constitutional procedures, its reliance on the established judicial system, and its recognition of the state's role as a vehicle for serving its people—that explains the success of the Shea Bill in the Massachusetts legislature.

The Bill was heard in Committee in mid-February and reported favorably by the Joint Legislative Committee on the Judiciary on March 11, 1970. It was passed by the Senate on March 24. Although it encountered more resistance within the House, it was passed, and survived a reconsideration vote. On April 2 the Bill was signed into law by the governor. Since that date similar measures have been introduced in the legislatures of several states, and the Shea Bill has opened a national discussion and reappraisal of basic questions concerning not only the war in Southeast Asia but also concerning the Constitution and relations between the branches of government.

I suspect that, like myself, many members of our legislature take pride not only in the fact that the Shea Bill originated in Massachusetts, but also in the fact that it was the product of legislative effort from the time Reverend Wells and Representative Shea first filed their Bill to its final passage. It was an example of legislative initiative and leadership, and as such stands as a special moment for those associated with its passage.

Shortly before his death, Jim Shea and I spoke to twenty-five thousand people gathered on the Boston Common to support our efforts to obtain a referendum in Massachusetts on the war issue and to protest President Nixon's action in sending American troops into Cambodia. It was not an easy day for either of us, and Jim particularly felt the ravages of dissatisfaction. There were those on both sides of the issue who arbitrarily and angrily rejected his effort to make dissent effective and to keep it within the existing system.

On one side there were those who considered dissent of any kind on the issue of the war as subversive and as serving only to undermine traditionally established and accepted value. On the other side there were those who equally were arbitrarily convinced that our system is so rigid and unresponsive that attempts to work within it are worthless and serve only to distract attention from the more radical changes they are seeking.

In a time of polarization such as ours, the path of creative and responsible dissent is not an easy one. Jim Shea took the lead in opposition to the war and to our national policies at a difficult time in our state. Those of us associated with him were aware of the burden he carried and the tensions it involved.

Whatever the decision of the courts in regard to the Shea Bill in this turbulent year, it gave an effective and responsible focus in a constitutional context in opposition to the war in Southeast Asia. It raised important and serious questions. And, as Jim Shea predicted, it helped once again to "establish Massachusetts as the nation's leader in protecting our constitutional heritage." In doing so, it gave our Legislature a moment for which we are proud. It also gave us added reason for being grateful to Jim Shea and for appreciating how much we in the General Court, and the people of Massachusetts generally, have lost now that he is no longer with us.

12   A Housewife Becomes Political

Sharon Scofield

A Government can manipulate its people only to the extent that they allow themselves to be manipulated.
                             —Sen. Joseph P. Ward, Fitchburg rally
                                        February 18, 1970

There must be a multi-issue approach to the problems that confront this country. All available ways of reaching our leaders must be used: mass protest, marches, political action, letters, telegrams, education of uncommitted Americans, and personal resistance, such as draft- or tax-resistance.

It was these feelings that led to my involvement with the Shea-Wells Bill. And it was my first opportunity to see our political system from the inside. Previous to this time I had avoided electoral politics entirely, with the exception of voting in a city election in which none of my candidates won. I am a housewife and the mother of a five-year-old son. I come from the South and my family's politics were verbally very conservative, but these verbal convictions were rarely ever acted upon, even in national elections. My own political convictions were non-existent until several years ago. Since then my awareness of problems both within and without this country has deepened and turned from passive awareness to active involvement.

At the time of the Fitchburg rally I was working with an anti-war group, the Beacon Hill Support Group for Vietnam Peace Action, which seeks to educate people about our government's involvement in Indochina. I was also active in a tax-resistance group, Boston War Tax Resistance.

My involvement in tax-resistance is more a personal act of conscience than a group activity. One of the government's main ways of manipulation is economic. As a citizen I am obligated to pay my taxes, but a major portion of my taxes goes to programs I cannot support. Thus I am in a position of paying for wars that are morally unsupportable, and at the same time seeing desperately needed domestic programs go unfinanced. Tax-resistance is an answer to this form of economic manipulation: Money should be withheld from the war to support neglected domestic programs.

My involvement in so many different areas may seem like an ineffective distribution of my time and energies, but I believe that there are many roads leading to peace and good government. We are being manipulated in many ways, and necessarily we must work in many ways to fight this manipulation. The most direct loss of power is in the political system. The Shea-Wells Bill offered people another opportunity for regaining some of that power while at the same time re-establishing constitutional authority in our government. I will confess that in the beginning I was not particularly optimistic about our chances for success, but before I wrote off our political system permanently I wanted to give it a chance.

I resent any form of governmental manipulation and Senator Ward's statement in Fitchburg suddenly brought into focus my reasons for working within the system on House Bill 2396. The impotence that most Americans feel, with regard to their power to influence government policy, is a direct result of their abdication of their rights and neglect of their duties as citizens in a participatory democracy.

I have no doubt that we are being manipulated by our government, but that can be stopped if we care enough to gain back the power that we, as citizens, hold over our elected officials.

But I am only one person and in order for the political process to respond, more people had to become involved. This meant educating people to the real facts of our government's policies.

My work on the Shea-Wells Bill had much to do with such an educational effort. It involved reaching out to people by telephone, radio, or in person: people in large groups or one at a time; talking to them about the Bill and why it was so important for them to become involved, urging them to write or call their state representatives and state senators in support of our Bill. I also helped set up a state-wide telephone tree to reach peace groups throughout Massachusetts.

Later on there was extensive petitioning to convince specific legislators who voted against the Bill on the first vote in the House of Representatives to change that vote. This was particularly gratifying to me as my own state representative was one of those who originally opposed the Bill. But large numbers of his constituents signed our petitions or personally called, wrote, telegraphed, or visited him asking that he reconsider. He responded by changing his vote and remarking that it was a pleasant change to hear from so many of his constituents on an issue. Here was our legislative system at its best. My faith in our system of government was rapidly being restored.

And finally we saw the culmination of everyone's efforts—the signing into law of House Bill 2396. The Shea-Wells Bill had made it. For me, who had never even dabbled my little finger in government, it was an amazing revelation. It could work! Our government—of, by, and for the people—could be just that. All it takes is people participating in their democracy.

I believe that we Americans are now reaping a harvest of long years of political apathy, and that harvest is the unrest, violence, and polarization of Americans that we see everywhere in our society today, as a result of unresponsive and irrelevant government.

But now a new crop is being sown by striking students, concerned housewives, businessmen, teachers, doctors, truck drivers, soldiers, and farmers—by people from all walks of life. And the crop yield will be a government that is responsive to the needs of its people—all its people. And the ideal climate for this crop is active interest and participation on all levels of government. Instead of plows and hoes, the tools are telephones, telegrams, and letters to your elected officials.

It's hard to responsively represent a vacuum. The term "silent majority" is taken from Greek literature and it means the dead. Don't be dead to your government. SPEAK OUT! It's your world, Baby! But it's mine too, and your silence threatens *me*!

13   Working for Jim Shea

John A. Businger

I came to work for Jim Shea in early January, 1970, almost by pure
chance; at least I had not heard of what was later to be called the
Shea-Wells Vietnam Challenge Bill, even though it had been filed in
early December at the deadline for introducing Bills. I was in the
process of returning to Boston College Law School that January, my
attendance there having been interrupted by service in the Navy the
previous year. I was acquainted with Jim because he associated with
those legislators I most admired. I followed his voting record before I
left for the service, and when the question of the cut in the size of the
Massachusetts House became a dominant issue he placed himself for it.
I had the opposing viewpoint and one day in June, before I left for the
service, I ran into him outside the State library. We talked about the
issue for about twenty minutes, both of us giving the other arguments
neither one of us had considered before, and both walked away from
that meeting questioning our own positions.

When I returned from the service in September I ran into Jim
crossing a street near the State House and learned he had changed his
mind about the House cut and now opposed it. Our meeting over this
issue impressed me so much that when I looked for a legislator to work
with in December, I considered Jim first, because he lacked staff and
because by then we were quite friendly.

What finally determined that I would work for Jim was a chance meeting with Robert Murray, who had just taken a position with the attorney general after having been a key person in Kenneth P. O'Donnell's campaign for governor. Bob was in the law firm that included Dave Mazzone and Steve Moulton, both of them supporters of O'Donnell. I asked Bob which legislators supported Ken O'Donnell. His first response was, "Jim Shea." When I decided to personally file a Bill to abolish the state convention to make state politics more open to popular participation, I found that Jim and Ken O'Donnell had already filed such a Bill. Thus Jim and I had several interests in common, strengthening my desire to work for him. I did not know then that John Wells had gone through these same people in November and early December to introduce his own Bill. He had gone to Ken O'Donnell, to Dave Mazzone, and to Jim Shea, who agreed to sponsor the bill. It struck me as great coincidence that the very day I started to work for Jim in January, I found that Ken O'Donnell had also been a key element in the introduction of the Bill.

On my first day at work with Jim, I walked in on the opening working meeting attended by the author of the Bill, the Reverend John Wells of Lexington; an ardent advocate and spokesman, Prof. Steve Worth, whom John had met at the Lowell November 15 Moratorium; and, of course, Jim Shea. John and Steve immediately began to explain and defend the Bill even before the introductions were over. A few minutes' conversation convinced me that as a matter of constitutional law the point they were making—that a state could sue the national government or a servant of it—was an arguable one, even if it worked out later not to be totally sound. The key point was the necessary distinction between what the proposed Bill sought to do, i.e., to challenge the executive's power to send men to a war in the absence of what the Constitution seems to require—congressional declaration of war—and the challenging of the national government by a state in a case where the power of the national government is more explicitly set out by the Constitution and where perhaps there have been court rulings which decide questions that the State wishes to challenge after that fact. Clearly no court rulings had explicitly resolved into a rule that the executive could make war in the absence of what seemed to be a constitutional requirement of congressional declaration.

The interest I had in the Shea-Wells Bill was immediate, because for some time I had been searching for what role I could personally play in helping to end the war. Thus began the next few months in which our Bill, which seemed like a pipedream in January, became reality in

106

March and April and spread to other states, finally reaching the United States Supreme Court. It is impossible to describe the events and the emotions of the next few months in any kind of brief and totally rational fashion. But the key events and the key people can be sketched out.

Our first task was clear—to get as much attention focussed on the Bill as possible. That meant two things: to get the media to take notice and to get peace groups, church groups, political groups, and individual constituents organized to make the Bill their first priority. I learned very quickly that some of those who should have been most interested were not at all sure that this effort should be any more than a token one. There were other activities on the fire, election of peace candidates being one and Moratorium activities being another, which many felt took precedence. Others thought the Bill had no chance in the Legislature and if it by some small chance survived that test, that the courts would not treat it seriously enough to make the entire effort a worthwhile activity.

Jim and I agonized at length at the reluctance of some of those who we thought should have been in the first ranks of support. I contacted an old friend of mine, Dick Cauchi, executive secretary of CPP, and after filling him in I urged him to convince CPP to give this effort a first priority. I contacted another old friend, Dennis Kanin, at the Moratorium office. He had served as chairman of the College Democratic Clubs of Massachusetts (CDCM) in 1967, the year they held their national convention in Boston, an event we hosted and helped coordinate, and an event at which the main speaker was Senator Eugene McCarthy. Two weeks later McCarthy announced his candidacy for the Democratic nomination for President. In fact, the new movie, "America Is Hard to See," lists this event as the start of the McCarthy campaign. Also at the Moratorium office were Ray Dougan, coordinator of the Massachusetts Moratorium, and Joe Gebhardt, who had worked on the McGovern Commission for Party Reform the previous summer. In late January we held our first press conference and had our initial meetings of larger groups.

Looking back, it amazes me to realize how well organized we became in only two weeks, which is all we had between our first press conference and the public committee hearing on February 11. We were really only a handful doing the work of hundreds, calling everyone imaginable from every stratum of society: unions, churches, peace groups, broad-range political action groups, aroused individual citizens, lawyers, young and old, rich and poor. Fred King of Newton was especially invaluable, plastering Boston with handbills giving the time and date of the hearing.

In my opinion, it was the public hearing that passed the Bill—this public airing of legal opinion, of aroused and intelligent citizens, all ably directed by Jim Shea, before a patient committee chaired so smoothly by Sen. Joseph Ward.

The hearing demonstrated to the Judiciary Committee the well-reasoned approach of the Bill and of its sponsors. It showed to the press that this was a serious effort, which perhaps had a chance after all. And it showed to the proponents that success was indeed possible.

So many people had so much to do with putting on the hearing that it is impossible to list them all. John Wells, Steve Worth, and Jim Shea found the speakers and obtained supporting telegrams from those unable to attend. Jim Shea, John Wells, Steve Worth, Mike Tigar, and Larry Velvel gave expert persuasive testimony. David Lustig handled public relations, and Mary Ann Seitz coordinated all the activities. By the end of the day citizens had acquired the courage to stand at the microphone and give their own eloquent testimony. Some of them had never faced a microphone before.

That public hearing had a galvanizing effect on the committee, the press, the proponents of the Bill themselves, and the legislative leadership. This Bill, win or lose, was not going to sink without a fight the likes of which the State House had not seen; and this fact alone had a tremendous impact upon the sometimes cynical members of the House. They were talking in the halls about the Bill and the forces behind it. Once the action started it fed upon itself until by late February the Bill had become the one item other than the House cut that was getting constant attention from the Legislature. This establishment of a priority status for the Shea-Wells Bill was the key action in passing it and was the outcome of one event, the public hearing.

But to pass the Bill needed more than just a hearing. It needed the support of more citizens, it required the support of more legislators, and the Bill itself needed some rewriting to ward off possible objections on legal grounds. We had to do all this between February 11 and March 12. Jim and I travelled across the state to discuss the Bill before all kinds of groups. Sometimes Steve Worth would come along to deliver his usual masterful, deeply emotional, but hard-headed intellectual speech. John Wells and Jim made some joint engagements and John, a master at bringing people together on the Bill, would ensure that the event went smoothly.

I will never forget the night in Franklin, Massachusetts, when Jim was the guest of Reverend Daniels at a Rotary Club dinner. At the end of his speech, it was not at all clear whether Jim had won their minds because, of course, those present had not had the opportunity before to think about our proposal. But as the questions began, a distinguished-looking gentleman, whom I had noticed at the far end of the hall, rose and wistfully but determinedly said, "You know, my professor at Harvard Law would have been for this Bill." He was immediately followed by someone right in front of Jim who proclaimed "that you liberals should have been like this a long time ago." He was echoing the complaint that liberals did not pay enough attention to the Constitution and that our notion was an essentially conservative, restorative one. We knew from that night on that a mass of citizens were with us from all strata of society and that one did not need to be long-versed in anti-war activity to support our Bill. What that night did for Jim's confidence could not be overestimated, it had so great an effect.

During this period the Bill was still being rewritten. The final Bill was actually authored by several people. There was John Wells, the originator of the Bill and of the idea that the state could sue the federal government to bring about a decision on the validity of congressionally undeclared wars. There was Jim Shea, who used to listen critically and closely to all ideas and gather them together in his own mind, often doodling on a few papers on his desk. There was myself, who also listened to all ideas and often checked them out in some old constitutional law books a friend had, and put forth my own ideas. And, of course, there was the input from the constitutional lawyers and professors contacted by Steve Worth and John Wells. Joe Ward was especially helpful in drafting the second section on procedure. Several members of the Judiciary Committee, such as the House chairman and Jack Backman, tinkered with the language to refine it.

During early March we learned that we had the support of Speaker Bartley and Senate President Donahue. Thus while the Bill was not yet reported out of committee, we knew that their support, together with that of Senator Ward, Senate chairman, and Representative Cornelius (Connie) Kiernan, the House chairman, had narrowed considerably the odds on the Bill. Jim always used to say that "this Bill I thought had a remote chance when we started but now things are getting better." When Jim said this in early March, he had an extra smile because he knew that the Bill had a fighting chance now, but he never wanted to overplay the chances. We were cautious in private, but we were never reticent to exhibit our strength openly, in impressive endorsements or in making it quite clear to legislators that the people were on our side.

So from early March until the Bill passed in late March we really put the pressure on, never ruffling feathers—but it was there. Until February 25, when it was defeated, we had competition from the House cut Bill, especially in the news media. Yet our small group put more pressure on the legislators for our Bill than they got during the House cut session. Several legislators confessed to me that despite all the public attention given to the House cut, their mail and phone calls on the Vietnam Bill completely dwarfed the efforts made for the House cut legistlation.

After that initial, tense 116 to 110 vote not to kill the Bill on March 12, we continued the pressure over the weekend. We tried not only to get citizens to call their legislators, but also to determine who were closest to the legislator whose vote we wanted. Who, for example, knew the representative from the South Shore? Who were his contributors, his political allies? We tried every means of reaching the legislators we could think of. Jim and I camped out in the State House over the weekend and he called many of his colleagues, both to congratulate those who had voted with us and to put the issue as best as possible to those who had voted against us.

We discovered that legislators were perfectly willing to tell Jim of the calls they had received. One opponent was wavering when we called him. On Monday I heard from a friendly AFL-CIO lobbyist that this same legislator had come to him to tell him that he was finally with us. He reported receiving fifty calls that weekend, even though he lived far from the center of our operation near Boston. Legislators came in on Monday, March 16, declaring to each other that they had never seen anything like the citizen lobbying for our Bill. Later we were struck by the strange coincidence that March 12, the day of the first vote, was the second anniversary of the McCarthy success in New Hampshire, and that March 16, the day of the clinching vote, was the second anniversary of Robert Kennedy's entrance into the presidential contest.

During the last week of March, the only question left was whether Gov. Frank Sargent would sign the bill. Jim was convinced he had to. While Massachusetts is not the overwhelmingly "peace state" outsiders have claimed, Jim felt Sargent had to sign the bill even if his beliefs went the other way. Not to sign was probably politically dangerous, because Ken O'Donnell had supported it from the beginning. Other gubernatorial candidates had supported it too. Senator Donahue came out in favor in late February; Mayor Keven White of Boston announced his support March 16; and former Lieutenant Gov. Francis X. Bellotti had announced he supported the Bill in answer to a question on a March 13 radio show. All Sargent's opponents would take up the cudgel if the Bill failed only because of a gubernatorial veto.

But we were not sure and our natural pessimism about getting such a momentous Bill actually signed into law led even Jim to worry, on that final day, April 2, when we went down uninvited to witness the press conference. Adding to our worry was the floating rumor that Sargent had finally decided to veto the Bill. But these stories proved to be false. No matter what twists and turns took place in the inner offices of the governor, he signed the Bill the afternoon of April 2.

The rest of April we had one remaining task, to get the Bill known nationally so that other states would pass similar legislation, adding to the legal force of our Bill.

Jim, John, and Steve travelled to other states whenever they could help in getting a Bill introduced. Each legislature had its own personality and its own rules but we kept at it, going to New York, Ohio, and Illinois. We had great contacts in California. There we met with Rep. John Vasconcellos of San Jose, and Frank Olrich, his assistant, and with Rep. Bill Greene of Los Angeles. We also worked with Representative Mann of Illinois; Representative Tom Hill in Ohio and in the Minority Leader's Office there; Representative Richardson of Newark, New Jersey; and Rep. Norman Bersen of Pennsylvania. Every national columnist in the country, Mary McGrory, Flora Lewis, Roscoe Drummond, James Jackson Kilpatrick, Peter Hamill, Tom Wicker, followed the example of reporters like Bob Turner, Ken Campbell, Dave Nyhan, and Rich Gaines in Boston. They paid the attention due this Bill; they recognized as others admittedly did not, even after passage of the Bill, that this law would become a history-making challenge.

Ken O'Donnell was also instrumental in locating people for us to see in other states. When his friends around the country called him to ask what was going on, he referred them to us. We were trying to do on a national scale what we had done in Massachusetts; we tried to reach not only legislators, but influential people and groups and the average man. We enlisted the aid of the New Democratic Coalition at their national convention in Chicago, which Fred King and Dick Cauchi attended. We found that candidates wanted our Bill to campaign on. So by April 15, we had become a going concern with national connections, whereas only three short months before, I had been sitting with Jim, John, and Steve, who were trying to convince me they had an idea of merit.

What had happened in three months cannot be adequately explained by me, but the passion and the intelligence of many kinds of people had made a dream into a reality—above all the passion and the intelligence of Jim Shea. He had not thought of the idea, but he helped draft the Bill and directed the public hearing into a masterpiece. Jim had something else: a unique ability to get along with all kinds of people because he genuinely liked many kinds of people. He persuaded many to be with us, and he neutralized those who were against us. Even if their judgment withstood his assault, they saw our side because of his easy-going but serious manner.

This same style led the people of Massachusetts to really take to Jim when he spoke at the Boston Common on April 15 and at the State House rally on May 5. Here was a serious and passionate young politician who had a flair for communicating with the young but who at the same time could talk to a Rotary Club in an easy convivial manner, joke with an opponent in the House, and have a drink with the Newton Elks. Here was a young politician who when he said, as he always did, "I am in politics to perform some public service," meant it and people knew it. He had the ability to make people care and to get them involved.

Before a large crowd at Gardner Auditorium at the State House in Boston former Senator Ernest Gruening (D-Alaska) speaks in support of House Bill 2396.

112A

14   You Do What You Can

Nicholas Peck

I was drinking chocolate milk at midday in the dining hall of Marlboro
College in Vermont when my friend and schoolmate, Karen Wells,
approached me with the news that a Bill written by her father was to be
discussed in committee in Boston in a few days.

After she had explained the Bill I remember feeling that at last there
was a chance to tame the thundering B-52's that had been sprinkling
napalm and Massachusetts-designed-and-built anti-personnel bombs
upon Vietnam during the last nine years of my twenty-three years of
life.

For the last five years, ever since I got out of high school, I had been
acutely aware of the absurdities of the government's statements in
support of its war. In my mind the Vietnam war is an impotent gesture
by a dying society, whose governmental thinkers probably realized back
in 1958 that expansive, competitive capitalism would soon be unable to
function in a world that has at least tripled in population since whites
began evolving their "civilization" on North America several centuries
ago.

Having realized this they probably winked at each other, drank a few
beers, and decided, "Let's hold out as long as we can, brother."

Following this advice, the government (which probably and ignor-
antly believes that there is a future for American imperialism) decided

to take a stand in Vietnam against the dull and sad world force known as communism which is, no matter how dull and brutal (and remember that humans are often this way), the only force on Earth that offers any hope of establishing a system emphasizing cooperation instead of the system of competition promoted by the "free" world.

And so we went fighting into Vietnam.

Well, I am one of those young Americans who has spent a ridiculous amount of energy getting to and participating in peace marches and rallies, etc. But what else could I do? Automation and the condition of the economy have made me and those of my generation obsolete except as students, which is an unnatural and absurd role for most of us. So, protesting became the way of life or the hobby for many.

The trouble was that over these years I kept realizing that the war and what it represented was too important to be handled solely by us hobbyists and nihilists.

This is why Karen's message caused me to put down my chocolate milk (which is the one thing I really learned to enjoy back in the fifties; I was too young for Elvis) in order to telephone the *Boston Globe,* for which I was a correspondent. I remember telling some editor that even if the Bill should be branded as a loser it would be important to let the readers of New England know about this effort to exert judicial force against our country's genocidal war by means of a legislative act.

Later when I was back in Massachusetts during debate in the House on the Bill, I learned that my representative in the House, Mary Newman, was opposing it. I called her up and she explained that in her mind the passage of the Bill by no means ensured that the Supreme Court would hear the case. Further, she claimed that the court system might come under attack and lose the faith of the people if and when the Court did refuse. I acknowledged her arguments saying, however, that the Bill did maximize the possibility of a Supreme Court ruling on the constitutionality of the war. Also, I expressed the thought that it was far better to introduce this complicated and controversial issue into the existing governmental machinery rather than let it ferment in the streets. I imagine that she'll come around to this last view by the time she reads this.

As I write this there is still more energy, in the form of body heat, draining out of dead and dying soldiers in Southeast Asia, than there is being expended by U.S. District Court and Court of Appeals judges, senators, congressmen, and the President to end this war. The Wells-Shea Bill may change this.

15   A Touch of Magic

Robert L. Turner

For a long time I thought Jim Shea was somebody's flunky.

During 1969, the thin, bespectacled young man would shuffle into our State House office about once a week, handing out press releases. He never identified himself, or said very much, and we all assumed he was delivering material for the man in the releases, state Rep. H. James Shea, Jr. (D-Newton)—whoever that was. In the Massachusetts House, freshman representatives are easily overlooked among their 239 colleagues.

But Shea's anonymity was not to endure. On January 26, 1970, he called a press conference to announce that he would challenge the war-making powers of the President of the United States. Shea said the issues he would raise, "transcend the peace effort and extend to the very heart of our constitutional system." The press conference was sparsely attended and its content, regarded as bravado by some newsmen, was barely reported.

Two weeks later, on February 11, Ash Wednesday, the Bill was listed twenty-sixth on an agenda of forty-three measures to be given a public hearing by the Legislature's Committee on the Judiciary. Also on the list were Bills to strengthen the state's drunk-driving laws and to deal with parking tickets on rental cars. The committee adjourned to the largest hearing room in the State House, where more than eight hundred persons cheered their support for the Shea Bill.

What set the Bill on its way, however, was not the support of young people, but the impressive string of witnesses gathered by Shea, including former Alaska Sen. Ernest Gruening and constitutional lawyers from as far away as Illinois, Kansas, and California. The committee chairman said later he had not been so overwhelmed by a hearing in twenty years as a legislator.

During the two-month fight for the Bill, Shea did a remarkable job of confining his attention to the constitutional issue, which he believed was the only argument which might secure passage of the Bill.

Although young people and peace groups appeared in force at Shea's original press conference and at the hearing, Shea discouraged demonstrations or public agitation afterwards. He knew that the legislators, often conservative, might react negatively to such action. "The peace groups fully supported us," Shea said after the Bill had been signed into law, "but we wanted the thing handled in the most politically sagacious way."

When debate opened in the House, Shea was discouraged when one of his supporters tried to turn the Bill simply into a peace issue. Shea was further saddened when opponents responded that the Bill would provide aid and comfort to the enemy—a constitutional definition of treason. And he was genuinely hurt by some of the hate mail he received, but he answered his critics only briefly. "Our approach to foreign policy should not be set in Hanoi—it should be set in our state houses and on Capitol Hill," he said.

Then he insisted that the central question was not one of war and peace but of the proper, legal exercise of power. "This Bill represents the most serious constitutional issue confronting our society today," he kept repeating.

During debate, opponents charged that Democratic leaders were supporting the bill only in hopes that it would prove embarrassing to Gov. Francis W. Sargent, a Republican who might be pressured by the White House to veto it. Shea never denied that this might be one consideration for some Democrats, but he never used the argument himself. "All I can do is work for the Bill as hard as I know how," he told me. "If the political climate happens to be right, then that's fine."

Within weeks of his first press conference, Shea achieved sudden fame, and he always seemed a little uncertain how to respond to it. The result was that he buried himself in his work, frequently spending eighteen or twenty hours a day making phone calls, doing research, and writing speeches—and press releases which he continued to hand-deliver.

116

Shea always seemed a little reluctant to tackle radio and television, but he always did it in an effort to increase support for his Bill. He seemed nervous on the air, but was driven by the clear vision of what his Bill was all about, and what it could do.

While the Bill was being redrafted, I wrote a column citing the impressiveness of the public hearing and the businesslike manner in which the Bill was being redrafted. Although the legislative process is purposely inefficient, I said, this appeared to be one of those rare instances when a touch of magic brought all the elements into a smooth-running effort. The next time I saw Jim Shea, he referred to himself laughingly as "Touch-of-Magic Shea." He did it in such an engaging, bashful manner I could tell he was a little embarrassed.

During the fight for the Bill, Shea confined himself to the constitutional issue, but he was not unaware of the broad implications of the Bill and the wide attention it was receiving. In perhaps his only departure from the narrow, issues-only view, Shea opened the House debate by saying that, "the eyes of the nation are upon Massachusetts. The hopes of millions for the assertion of constitutional government rest with this House."

Other supporters of the Bill imbued their rhetoric with historical perspective. Several witnesses at the hearing invoked the memory of James Otis, Elbridge Gerry, and other colonial patriots. One senator said the Bill might conceivably end the war sooner; and if it did, he said, "we will have performed an act of simple greatness." And the Bill won its initial test in the House after one representative said, "We have the opportunity and the obligation to make some history here today."

But Shea rarely went in for the grandiose phrase. I continually tried to get him to say that the Bill's passage would be an act of patriotism unique in legislative history or an unparallelled act of heresy or whatever he thought. But Shea would never bite. After the Bill was signed, he said simply, "As both a legislator and a citizen, I am proud to say that the system has performed, and performed well."

Shea had not been sure the governor would sign the Bill. At the ceremony in which he did, Shea squeezed into a corner of the crowded room between one of the governor's aides and the American flag. He had in his pocket two brief statements, one to be released if the Bill were signed, the other for a veto.

Two weeks after the signature, Shea spoke to some fifty thousand people at a peace rally on Boston Common and expressed some pique that Governor Sargent was taking some of the credit for the new law.

Shea was heckled by a few radicals in the crowd, but he spoke candidly:

> There is much to despair about—much pressure to be cautious, which means to be silent. But we know this—if we are not silent the people will rally on our side against the war. We know this—the war will end and the system will change when, and only when, we compel it to. There is no one and nothing, when all is said, that can gag the voice of the people.

Hours later, a group of young radicals including some who had been at the Common rioted in Harvard Square. Weeks later, Jim Shea was dead. Within two days, someone had used a can of black spray paint on the gray pedestal of a Civil War memorial facing the State House. The black paint read, "Shea—He Lives."

16   Making the System Work

Mary Ann Seitz

I first became acquainted with the Shea-Wells Bill during the Fall of 1969. I worked with John Wells in Lexington on Moratorium activities during the months of September, October, and November. He mentioned occasionally the idea of using the state to challenge the constitutionality of the war. We were all so busy that none of us got terribly involved with or thought a great deal about his idea. During the planning meeting for the November Moratorium, John for the first time went into detail—the drafting of the bill, what wording would be used, and some of the constitutional arguments in favor of it.

Since we were primarily a group of Northern liberals, the reaction in the group was an amusing one. Many people felt that this was interposition, and John was a Georgia boy. You can take the man out of Georgia, but you can't take Georgia out of the man. The idea of using the state against the federal government, or interposing the state between the individual soldier and the federal government, smelled too much like the Southern doctrine. Shortly after the Moratorium, John called me and told me that he had found a state legislator who would be interested in his Bill and who would file it for him on request. Kenny O'Donnell had put John in touch with Jim Shea. John asked me at the time if I would work with him, since we had worked together well during the Moratorium.

119

In December, I went with John for the first time to Jim's office for a planning meeting. The Bill had been filed, and we decided that we were going to go all out on it. I was interested in the Bill because the feeling in November was quite different from that in October during the Moratorium. Once again those of us who felt very strongly about the Vietnam war were slipping back into apathy. The Bill appeared to be a vehicle, whether constitutional or not and whether passed or not, for the expression of the anti-war sentiments within the state.

During the course of the first meeting in Jim Shea's office, I met Steve Worth, John Businger, Ron Rosenblith, and of course Jim. The meeting was a little confused, since we didn't know each other. We spent the first half hour or so getting acquainted and throwing out ideas. From the meeting came the form of what we wanted to do immediately. We wanted, first, public exposure for the Bill. People would have to know via the press that the Bill had been filed, since many, many Bills are filed and lost every year. It was at this point that we decided to hold the first press conference. We also decided to make use of the lawyers' Moratorium list, a list of several thousand attorneys who had signed an ad in October calling the war illegal. We sent a massive mailing to them in the next two days, asking for their aid, aid in both time and money.

I was impressed by Jim Shea at the first meeting. We all talked, and we all threw out ideas. Jim listened very quietly. Toward the end of the meeting, he sat back in his chair and summed up what had happened at the meeting and those points which were useful. He did it concisely and with precision, and he did it with his sense of humor, which was a lovely one.

The response to the mailing was fair. We got some money and some offers of help. Probably the best offer was from a young man in the attorney general's office, who was an assistant attorney general, Bob Conlon, and who worked with us from that time forward.

David Lustig, who was to be our public relations expert, came to the second meeting in Jim's office. We worked out the details of the press conference and called all of the Boston media. The conference went well. John Wells, Jim Shea, and Steve Worth spoke, John and Steve going into the constitutional arguments, Jim talking about why he had decided not just to file the Bill on request, but to work actively for it. Shortly after that we started receiving mail, more mail than we expected, from the public.

The next week the big project was setting up the hearing. Senator Ward had been very cooperative; he said we would have a full hearing in Room 220 of the State House, a fairly small room that might hold a hundred people. We wanted to use Gardner Auditorium, which seats more than six hundred, and in fact it ended up that way. On the day of the hearing there were *hundreds* of people waiting outside the corridor. The crowd was orderly, polite, responsive. In every way it was a model hearing, what a legislative hearing ought to be. We were all very impressed by Senator Ward; he handled people with good humor and reason.

Media coverage of the hearing was good. Right from the beginning the *Boston Globe* was wonderful to us. We had an early editorial, which spoke of this Bill as being in the spirit of Henry David Thoreau, and the *Globe* from that time on celebrated us occasionally as making the system work.

After the hearing ended that evening, I rode up in the elevator with Representative St. Cyr of Millis, who said that when he came into the hearing he had felt that the notion was somewhat laughable. He now intended to vote in favor of the Bill because he had been very impressed by the constitutional arguments, by the atmosphere, and by the attitude of all the individual citizens who had come in to testify on behalf of the Bill. Also, some Massachusetts politicians had been expressing a doubt that the government was responsive to the people, and I think the Judiciary Committee members felt as proud as we did of that hearing. It was an elegant hearing.

During the time that the Judiciary Committee was considering the Bill, we printed leaflets giving the members' names, addresses, and phone numbers. We distributed probably about forty thousand of these through the various organizations within the state, with excellent results. Senator Ward has said that he received more phone calls on this than on any other issue; people stopped him on the street and in the corridors of the State House and asked him to work for it and to vote for it.

After word came out about the positive committee report, we started our lobbying efforts on the House. This was probably the most intense period of the entire course of the Bill. I was on the phone eight to ten hours a day, calling all over the state, calling groups, individuals, friends, friends of friends, relatives, getting people to call their state representatives and tell them that they wanted this thing done, that they wanted an avenue for constitutional challenge.

The first vote was a very close one, 116 to 110. It came on Thrusday. We knew they would be voting again early the next week, so that weekend was going to be the crucial weekend. We went through the list of representatives, the people from the Speaker's office, those who could be swayed, those whom we could sway, those whom the Speaker could sway. We singled out vulnerable people on the list who had voted with us who could be pressured over the weekend and people who had voted against us whom we probably could bring over to our side with a little pressure. We worked very hard that weekend.

One representative on Beacon Hill, named Moe Fry, had approximately five hundred calls between Thursday night and Monday morning. He was on the phone continually. Another representative, Mary Newman in Cambridge, a Quaker, received the same treatment. She later said that she had not had time to have meals, because whenever she attempted to cook something the phone would ring and her food would burn. She never did vote with us. Our own representative in Lexington was against us. We worked on him all weekend. We sent a delegation of distinguished Lexington citizens to him, people who had in the past worked in his campaigns or given him money. He maintained until early Monday morning that he was still against us. Then he voted with us on the floor. He had responded to the pressure, which had been intense. We made it through the House. Our work had done a lot of good. We had a good generous margin.

Sitting in the gallery during that time, we enjoyed ourselves thoroughly. The proponents of the Bill had done their homework. They had been at the hearing and were thoroughly versed by constitutional experts on the meaning of this Bill. The opponents had done very little work. They were reacting in a surface way to the Bill. There were statements about Hanoi watching the State House, which made the gallery giggle, and made the Speaker gavel us down and tell us we'd all have to leave if we were going to giggle any more. One man stood and said he didn't understand why we were talking about Vietnam when there were sex offenders all over the streets. We giggled again, and got gaveled down again. Representative Connie Kiernan, who led the floor fight in the House, did a beautiful job. When everything became too emotional, when there were times when people would talk about the boys who had been wounded in Vietnam and were being abandoned by the state, Kiernan would stand and say that his concern was for these same boys and that they go to a war that is supported by the country. He kept things from degenerating entirely into emotional arguments.

We went into the Senate next. The atmosphere there was entirely different, partly because the opponents had done their homework. Their arguments were also from the constitutional point of view. However, in many ways, the Bill was now practically passed. It had gone through the House with a large enough vote so that it seemed inevitable, and we had the support of the Democratic leadership in both the House and the Senate.

After the vote in the Senate, we waited a short while for the governor to sign it, hoping that he would add the emergency preamble so that the Bill would not have to wait ninety days to be a state law. The governor did add the preamble, and the Shea-Wells Bill became law in the state of Massachusetts.

From this point on, the Bill really belonged to the attorney general and the Supreme Court. We spent some of our time getting information to other states and to interested parties who wanted to attempt either to pass this Bill or to get it on their ballots in their states. Most of my time at this point was spent working with Jim and talking with him about where he wanted to go from here. I did not want him to run for Secretary of State. He seemed to be vacillating between that and running again for representative or for senator.

I saw Jim last the Wednesday before his death. He asked me what I thought he should do, and I repeated, run for either representative or senator. We talked a little bit about some of the young people who were running. Later in the week, on Friday, I talked for a short moment to Jim. We were both rushed and said very little except that we would see each other the next day at the CPP convention, where CPP intended to endorse Jim for Secretary of State. He asked me again if I thought he should do it, and I said no.

My father called me at six o'clock the next morning to tell me that he had been out in the car and thought he'd heard something about Jim Shea's being dead. My husband called the *Globe*, and they said, yes, he'd been shot the night before. I called a couple of the people who had worked with us to tell them, and then John Wells called me to tell me that there would be a memorial service at the convention and that we should all go out and then come to his house. We spent that day together, and some of the next day, but there didn't seem to be very much for anybody to say. We were all very hurt and very lost. Jim was a big loss, not just to his friends, but to everybody, to those people who would have been his friends, and to those people who would have been represented by him, represented in a way that few politicians are capable of.

The group had worked together worked as a unit, almost as one person. We started together with a few ideas, and the ideas grew and they worked, and we became overwhelmed by the Bill. Everything else got lost—our home lives, our jobs, our work—and we lived the Shea-Wells Bill probably twelve hours a day, and our families and employers were kind enough to let us do it.

17 A Question Still to Be Answered

Kenneth O'Donnell

Dr. John Wells introduced me at the Peace Rally in October. I was deeply impressed, not just by his words but by the obvious sincerity and compassion and manner in which they were delivered. His love for his country and its principles shone clearly, and his belief that dissent and differences should be freely exposed with reason and fairness was apparent.

A few days after our meeting on that cold October evening, John Wells came to me from a community of interest. He spoke eloquently of his devotion to spending all of his efforts and time to bring to an end this ugly confrontation in Southeast Asia. With the Moratorium behind him, his fertile mind had again thought of another way in which he could continue to prod the American consensus to cease this waste of our blood and treasure in a far-off land. With his deep religious conviction, he saw the moral posture of the United States, this great and wonderful land, being morally compromised. He was the father of what was called the Shea Bill.

He came to me as one who had long and arduously opposed this conflict, and he sought my help. He asked if the so-called political system did not provide an avenue of debate and dialogues and peaceful dissent. He said he had sought fruitlessly to pursuade any legislator to place before our elected representatives legislation that would prod their consciences and through them the consciences of the peace-loving citizens, not just of Massachusetts but of this nation.

He sought to raise a serious constitutional question as to whether any man, even the President, could arbitrarily declare the United States at war. Mr. Shea was there. He rose to the task. The issue was joined. H. James Shea, Jr. is no longer with us, but the torch he lit still burns and the question he asked remains to be answered.

18   The Story Moves Nationally

Richard Gaines

In January while nothing much of interest was happening at the State House, a freshman representative whose name I did not know called a news conference. I didn't attend, writing the event off as more insignificance. Any news coming from the conference, I assumed, would reach me sooner or later. When it ended, I was sitting at my typewriter as reporters who had covered the news conference began drifting back to the press gallery.

One writer for a suburban daily was talking about state Rep. H. James Shea, Jr., who had called the news conference. "He's got a lot of nerve," this writer said. "I asked him if he had sought the advice of House counsel in drafting the Bill, and you know what he said?" the writer asked. "He said he didn't need to. He said he had excellent advice from leading attorneys. Can you imagine that?" the writer said, answering his first question and posing another which required no reply.

That's how it all started for the press—as a Bill so steeped in indifference that no one took the time to think about its implications. By the time Gov. Francis W. Sargent signed the Shea-Wells Bill more than two months later, it had grown into a national story of great significance.

Following the news conference, little attention was given the Bill until a public hearing on it before the Joint Legislative Judiciary Committee on February 11. The public hearing was a great organizational achievement and, from the media's viewpoint, represented a turning point for the Shea-Wells Bill. Gardner Auditorium in the sub-basement of the State House was jammed with about eight hundred supporters of the Bill. They were of all ages and had various amounts of hair. The television cameras were there to record the event. The committee, headed by intellectual state Sen. Joseph D. Ward, a Democrat from Fitchburg, sat seriously while Wells, Shea, Prof. Steve Worth, and former United States Sen. Ernest Gruening of Alaska began building their case for the Bill.

Gruening's appearance was pivotal. Not only was his testimony excellent news copy through its far-reaching indictments of the Johnson Administration and his reflections on the reactions in Congress to the alleged Gulf of Tonkin incident, but it gave what would have been only a state-wide story a strong national appeal.

Although the aging, white-haired Democrat made little reference to the Bill itself except to endorse it, others did. They hit hard on the potential the Bill held for changing the power balance between Congress and the President. And at the same time, they took great pains to explain that the legislation in no way raised the issues of states' rights or nullification.

As witness upon witness urged the committee to report the Bill favorably, as witness upon witness explained that the Bill questioned only the legality of conducting a war in the manner the United States was conducting the Vietnam war, and as witness upon witness said he felt the United States Supreme Court could be induced to rule on the questions raised by the Bill, my boredom with the story gave way to waves of excitement.

Here was the making of an important news story, I said to myself as I sat in the hearing room. At 11:30 a.m., I ran across the street to my UPI bureau to file a short story for afternoon newspapers. At 2:30 p.m., I wrote a longer story for the next day's morning newspapers. The second story moved nationally.

Although many writers had become convinced of the Bill's unique qualities by this time, they remained skeptical about its legislative future. I was among them. The story had yet to reach the front pages. It was during the following week that word leaked from Ward, himself an attorney and a former Boston University Law School professor, that

128

the committee would redraft part of the Bill and report it favorably to the House. That information marked the first indication that the lawmakers were taking the Bill seriously. The skepticism was giving way to serious consideration. About this time, the political leaders of both parties—Republican Gov. Francis W. Sargent and Democrats Maurice A. Donahue, the president of the Senate, and David M. Bartley, the Speaker of the House—for the first time began assessing the political implications of the Bill.

All this activity took place while the Bill was still in the Judiciary Committee and augured the dramatic events still to come. Without doubt, the public hearing had been the turning point.

Public hearings, theoretically, serve an intelligence-gathering function in the legislative process. It is at public hearings that proponents and opponents of different Bills express their feelings concerning legislation. Once again, theoretically, the information gathered at public hearings is used by committee members to determine whether the Bill should receive a favorable or an unfavorable report.

But in practice almost without exception, committee hearings serve only as safety-valve outlets for public opinion, as cynical efforts to convince the people their views do count. But what happens, once again in practice almost without exception, is that the committee carefully considers the political pressures exerted by lobbying interests—all of this in the privacy of executive sessions—and issues its report to the House or Senate, which more often than not abides by the committee action.

But the Shea-Wells Bill was an exception in every respect. In a way, it proved the system could work as it was designed to work, which coincidentally was an argument used by supporters of the Bill: that it was a means of working effectively within the system.

The hearing helped coalesce public and legislative opinion behind the Bill and at the same time helped focus media attention on it. For a foreign-policy Bill with high philosophical content that itself made the Bill unique in a state legislature, such results were crucial to its eventual success. Ward said more than once how impressed he was with the case made for the Bill at the public hearing. Before the hearing, the Bill was an interesting freak. Afterwards, it was an item to be reckoned with in one way or another. And that's what public hearings are for, political scientists tell us.

When the Bill reached the House floor for its first and by far most important test, the press galleries were jammed with newsmen, many of whom had supported the measure privately. No one was confident of the vote until it was actually recorded on the electronic tote boards on either side of the sprawling House chamber.

When Speaker Bartley announced the razor-thin 116-110 margin in favor of the Bill, cheering erupted in the visitor's gallery. It drowned out muffled sighs of relief uttered by more than a few newsmen, myself included. And we reporters began asking ourselves, what would the Republican governor do with the Bill?

For the next week as the Bill moved through the House and Senate, newsmen took spare moments to ruminate about Sargent's decision. Rumor had it that his staff was close to evenly split over the Bill with about half opting for the governor to sign it and the rest opting for a veto.

No one was able to get any hard word out of Sargent's office until April 2, the day set aside for a news conference to announce a decision. That morning, word filtered out that Sargent had been planning to sign the Bill but that in the waning hours before 3 p.m., the time set aside for the announcement, those opposed to the Bill had gained the upper hand. It appeared to me from rumors that the governor would reject it. Shortly after noon, I bumped into Jim Shea in the halls outside the fourth floor press gallery. He told me he did not know what Sargent would do with the Bill, but that he was less confident than he had been at the start of the day.

Since that day, I have been unable to verify any of the assumptions and rumors related above. Thus, to me at least, they remain speculation or perhaps something stronger that has no name. Not until I received a news release at exactly 3 p.m. from Carl Cedarquist, a state trooper assigned to the governor, did I know that Sargent would sign the Bill.

Grabbing the two-page statement, I ran to the press gallery one flight up to file a bulletin by telephone for any afternoon newspapers still able to take the story. I learned later that some newspapers west of the Eastern time zone received the word in time to place the bulletin in their last editions.

Earlier in the day, I had prepared two bulletins, one that Sargent had vetoed the Bill and another that he had signed it. I was too nervous to be happy that he had done the latter, and because of the confusion that always seems to surround a big, breaking story, I don't remember what my counterpart for the Associated Press was doing. I presume he was filing a similar bulletin about the same time as I.

My wife, who is also a writer, remained at the news conference to take down quotes. When I returned to the third floor Executive Council chamber after filing the story, the news conference was still in progress. It was hot as hell in the small room since television lights had been on for close to forty-five minutes. The room was jammed with about one hundred writers, legislators, staff members, and miscellaneous observers. Within the hour, Atty. Gen. Robert H. Quinn, a Democrat, called his own news conference to announce plans to bring a test case under the new law before the United States Supreme Court.

It seems that everyone gets into the act on such politically loaded issues. In a way, in fact, that was what the Shea-Wells Bill was all about. The Bill entered the political scene with no significant support. With increasing coverage from the media, however, it soon became an issue on which all politicians were virtually compelled to take a stand. Once major figures in the Democratic Party began pushing the Bill, the rest of the political community fell into line. At its moment of truth, few politicians wanted to buck the rising tide of public opinion in support of the Bill. If nothing else, the history of the Shea-Wells Bill showed the heights to which government is capable of rising when the political climate is right.

Of those legislators who voted for the Bill, a significant number did so reluctantly under prodding from Bartley and Donahue. Once reported out of committee, the Bill became a pivotal political issue in an election year. And fortunately for Shea, Wells *et. al.,* it was the Democratic legislative leadership which first sought to exploit or use the measure, for it is the Democrats who control both the House and Senate with an iron hand. Goaded by strong editorial support from the *Boston Globe* among other newspapers, Bartley and Donahue cast themselves as front-line peace-men through their support for the Bill. If they were not, and we may never know for sure, the question is academic. How they behaved was more important to this tale.

Had Sargent vetoed the Bill, he would have been cast in the role of a Nixon Republican in a state that gave Hubert Humphrey his largest victory margin over Nixon in the 1968 presidential election, and at the same time he would have established a sharp contrast between himself and the Democrats, thereby producing an important campaign issue for the November gubernatorial campaign.

All four Democrats who sought to unseat Sargent, including Senate President Donahue, had endorsed the measure by the time it reached the governor's desk. Political polls at the time showed Sargent running far ahead of all four Democrats, leaving him in a quite enviable position. He would have gone a long way, I'm guessing, to maintain that position. In April, that meant signing the Bill.

There is no doubt that political expediency played a major role in the successful history of the Shea-Wells Bill. But so what? If political expediency is capable of improving the performance and responsiveness of elected officials, that's how the political system is supposed to work.

I should say, however, that the political climate for this unique situation was owed at least in part to the role of the media, which if slow-moving to adopt the issue at the start, eventually made the Bill an unavoidable issue by focussing state and national attention on it. Once that was done in a political climate turned toward peace by Massachusetts' powerful anti-war community, the legislators and the governor had little difficulty discerning the most propitious course to take.

It was almost as if you had read about this story long ago in a junior high school civics book on how government works. It may not happen very often but when it does, ah, Democracy in action—what a lovely sight.

19   The Issue Is Joined

Governor Francis W. Sargent

There were some who thought it the better part of prudence for me to ignore Vietnam Moratorium Day, October 15, 1969. There was the risk of demonstrations, of disruption—and there were possible political consequences for a Republican governor with a Republican President in the White House.

I decided to go because I had something to say. These were my words on Lexington Green that day.

> I am here today in conscience. I am here as a man who knows war in awful intimacy, a man who has fought a war. I am here to say the war in Vietnam must end. This war is costing America its soul. The battle for freedom in Vietnam must be fought by those whose freedom is at issue—the people of Vietnam themselves. Across America today we speak to our leaders that they may know our will. Some say the President is not listening. I say the President *is* listening. I have come to tell you what I am saying to him. The war in Vietnam must end. I say the President *is* listening to what America says today. If our voice is as one, that voice will be heard and the action that results will bear witness to that voice. I say—don't give up on the President of the United States. No man in America can speed the end of this war more than he. We must help the man who leads this nation toward the goal we all seek. The end of the war in Vietnam. We must unite in strength and resolution, join in moral force, from White House to Lexington Green, to restore this nation to the spirit of its youth.

My appearance on Lexington Green provided a background for a speculation that began months later as the so-called anti-Vietnam war Bill began its progress through the Massachusetts Legislature.

Many believed I would do everything to keep the Bill from reaching my desk, because it would embarrass me politically: The White House would want the measure defeated, the theory went, and would look to me to veto the Bill; on the other hand, given Massachusetts' strong liberal constituency, I would be pressed to sign it.

Privately, I had little doubt I would sign the Bill if it reached me and publicly I declined any comment on the measure, wishing to avoid interference with the legislative process. Our legal staff began review of the Bill while I told members of the Republican leadership in the Legislature that they and their fellow legislators should vote their conscience on the measure without reference to any real or imagined political embarrasssment the governor might risk.

I kept an open mind on the Bill as it moved through the Legislature, with amendments offered, considered, rejected and the Bill taking final shape. The speculation mounted that I would veto the Bill for political reasons.

A week before the Bill was finally enacted and sent to me, I was in Washington for a White House meeting. During the visit, I was briefly in the President's office on another matter and left behind a short memo outlining the intent of the legislation, explaining its progress through the legislature, and indicating that, while it was likely some of its backers were relishing the prospect of embarrassing me politically with the issue, others of its sponsors were obviously sincere, and, legally doubtful though the measure was, I would likely sign it.

I was thanked for the information and I left the White House.

The President had, on other occasions, made clear that he understood the governor of a state finally had to make decisions alone. It was apparent to me he felt this way in this case.

By the time the Bill formally reached the Governor's Office, my staff had been debating the subject for days and the lines of opinion were clear between those who were convinced the Bill was unconstitutional and should be vetoed, and those who believed the question it posed deserved attention, and that the Bill should be signed.

My decision came easily—and with these words, at 2:00 p.m., April 2, 1970:

I am today signing S. 5165—a measure of sincere intent, doubtful effect.

The intent: to present our highest tribunal with the grave question of whether and under what circumstances an individual can be required to serve in an armed conflict that lacks a formal congressional declaration of war. In these times, few questions have equal gravity, few warrant more serious consideration.

The effect: uncertain and in considerable dispute. It is asserted this measure, seeking to grant rights to Massachusetts citizens that would not be granted to other Americans, is doomed to a federal court judgment of unconstitutionality that would preclude consideration of the larger question: the validity of a congressionally undeclared conflict.

Yet the sponsors of the measure seek no less a judgment than that of the U.S. Supreme Court—and I will not stand in the way of that quest.

I therefore choose neither to express my own judgment, nor seek that of our attorney general, nor even that of our own Supreme Judicial Court.

I sign this measure to permit its sponsors to seek their day in our nation's highest court.

I am moved to make these observations.

False hopes may be raised by this measure's passage, hopes in the hearts of many parents of draft-age young men that it will safeguard their sons from conflict's peril. This measure's legal development may be lengthy and, as I have indicated, its result doubtful. Hope should be tempered with caution and realism. Further, Massachusetts servicemen should realize this Bill's enactment provides no license for them to disobey lawful orders received from military authorities.

False issues have been raised in this measure's debate.

The issue is not America's foreign policy in Southeast Asia, not whether a specific declaration of war is desirable in Vietnam, not whether advocates or opponents of this Bill are politically motivated, not—emphatically—whether the loyalty to the United States of any participant in this debate is questionable.

The issue, I repeat, is whether and when, under our Constitution, a citizen can be compelled to engage in a conflict that lacks a congressional declaration of war.

That issue is valid. Indeed, it is one of life or death.

Its resolution, treated in that spirit, is neither to be feared nor avoided.

I sign this measure in that conviction and in order that such a resolution not be delayed I cause the measure to take effect immediately.

House Speaker David M. Bartley (D-Holyoke) signs Shea-Wells Bill.

20 Two Concerned Citizens

Elizabeth and Stillman Williams

What was the magic of the Shea Bill? What were its inner strengths to meld citizen response and to sustain momentum for successive legislative steps?

For us, two features were paramount: First, there was no ambiguity as to immediate goal; and second, there was little ambivalence as to values. In the words of the *Boston Globe* editorial of January 30, 1970, "If the spirit of Thoreau should so move the Legislature to pass it [the Shea Bill], this little pebble cast on the water could make some mighty big waves."

We were pleased to have been invited in at an early stage—midday of December 2, John Wells phoned to ask, "Would we be willing to join on a quick trip to Boston to meet a Bill-filing deadline?" The deadline was met.

Wheels really began to roll in late January: typing, duplicating numerous letters, news releases, drafts of the Bill, plus a State House news conference, and an at-home dinner when we were privileged to introduce John Wells and Charlie Whipple.

The real push, in early February, was for a thousand copies of Steve Worth's twenty-six page brief. Betty Loomis helped me type a stencil, and two night sessions for us in the First Parish Church mimeograph room completed the run. The brief was collated at the Church by assistants of all ages in time for immediate mailing.

It was particularly gratifying and heartening to see, hear, and feel the eloquent testimony and the response at the February 11 Judiciary Committee hearing. This was the involvement of people, working within the framework of the democratic and legislative process. This was the thrust noted in meetings, then and later, and in talking to many people in the legislative galleries. Here in Lexington, it drew many persons together—in the First Parish Church, in the community, in initiative actions by the people of the community, in supplementary petition by town meeting members—to communicate to members of the legislature and to the governor. It was the message of the *Boston Globe* Thoreau editorial coming true.

Let us hope that the Shea Bill can become a beacon, a fulcrum for meaningful peace as national policy, to help create a world of law, justice and freedom, a world matured to universal citizenship and enfranchisement, and a world of health and joy in anticipation of a more safe, sane, and dependable tomorrow.

21   The Massachusetts Vietnam Bill

Jack H. Backman

A Reaffirmation of Constitutional Government

The Joint Judiciary Committee of the Massachusetts Legislature is composed of twenty-one members of the Massachusetts House of Representatives and Massachusetts Senate, sitting jointly to consider legislation relating to the judicial process. The "Vietnam" Bill filed by Rep. H. James Shea, Jr. and Rev. John Wells attracted little attention when it was filed in routine manner in December, 1969. It was referred to the Judiciary Committee, and the initial reaction of legislators who came in contact with the Bill was that it was of little note, a strange product, and one that would be routinely recommended to oblivion. The first notice of the Bill, as far as many legislators were concerned, was not by persons espousing passage, but by bitter and vehement opponents who had somehow been notified that a "radical" kind of measure was being considered by the Legislature. Without understanding the content, many individuals were calling their legislators and demanding to know if there was any possibility that our Legislature would be so foolish as to pit the Commonwealth of Massachusetts against the federal government and refuse to stand among the fifty states in defense of our nation.

It was under such unfavorable beginnings that the Judiciary Committee received the Bill for consideration.

The Bill was one of a number of matters assigned for hearing at the same time, and as the time approached, it was apparent that the Committee hearing room, which can seat no more than seventy to one hundred persons, would not be large enough for those attending. The hearing was therefore adjourned to the newly constructed Gardner Auditorium where eight hundred citizens poured in to fill all the seats.

The Committee Chairman, Sen. Joseph Ward, called the meeting to order with the announcement in well-modulated tones that this hearing was going to be conducted fairly and completely, that every person wishing to speak would have full opportunity, but that there would not be allowed any outbursts of applause or discord, and that any persons violating the rule would be summarily ejected.

The hearing was conducted in just that manner from two o'clock in the afternoon until seven o'clock that evening when the last person who wished to speak completed his testimony. Although many of the speeches were filled with emotion, the audience filling the large auditorium to capacity sat in almost complete silence throughout the hearing. There were no recesses and the testimony was uninterrupted, except by occasional questions of members of the committee.

At the close of the hearing, there was spontaneous applause by the audience for the manner in which it had been conducted by the chairman and the committee, and many members of the audience came up to the podium to congratualte the members of the committee.

It must be stated that the hearing itself, conducted in this fashion, had an almost stunning effect upon the members of the Judiciary Committee. At the time of the hearing, the writer was the only member of the committee to have placed himself in favor of the measure. So strong was the impact of the hearing, that the committee filed a unanimous report favoring passage of the Bill.

The key to the success of the United States system of constitutional government is the fundamental and pervading notion from its beginnings that we are a nation of laws and not of men (*Marbury* v. *Madison,* 1803).

It might be appropriately mentioned that the basic theme of the far right in their cry for law and order is that there must be a basic respect and submission to law if our society is to survive or progress. Yet how can this basic respect and reverence for law be established in a society where such large numbers believe that the chief executive has himself gone beyond the powers of the Constitution in pursuing an illegal war?

Today, any talk about the aspirations, the goals, or the ideals of government must of necessity begin with an end to the Vietnam war. This is a prerequisite to progress, an unsurmountable obstacle to our nation.

We as a nation shall not regain among either our youth or the nations as a whole a spirit of respect for law, reverence and compassion for humanity, or pride in government until this cancer is eradicated.

A government of laws and not of men also means that no man, in whatever office, shall, for indefinite periods of time, suspend, cancel, or nullify the law of this great land. It is from this approach that we should now examine the problem of the Vietnam Bill.

We must first lay a little ground work as to law. First, neither the President nor Congress has untrammeled authority over citizens in time of peace or in time of war. There have been cases delineating and defining the limits of authority of both the executive and the legislative branches of our government. This has been done, always with great reluctance and with reserve by the United States Supreme Court, the third branch of our government. The very fundamental case of law in this nation, which had no parallel in any other nation in the world up to that time, was the case of *Marbury* v. *Madison, supra,* when Chief Justice Marshall of a Supreme Court that was less than thirty years old, had the temerity, perhaps the gall, but without doubt the inspired vision and foresight to make a declaration in the name of the nine-member United States Supreme Court that the legislature of the United States Congress, duly elected by the people of this nation that had just fought a revolution to elect the Congress, had in fact acted beyond the powers of the Constitution. An act of the elected national legislature of the people had gone beyond its powers! Could the Supreme Court tell the Congress that it was acting beyond its powers? It did, and since that time we have attempted to carry out a system of rule of law and not of men—*even congressional men or presidential men.*

Now, what are the laws and what are men? In this case, the law is our Constitution. It gives the power to command our armed forces to the President. It gives the power of foreign policy to our President. It gives the treaty power to the President in conjunction with Congress. It gives broad implied powers to the President to act in cases of emergency. By acts of Congress of February 28, 1795 and March 3, 1807, the President is authorized to call out the militia and use the militia and naval forces of the United States in case of invasion by foreign nations, and to suppress insurrection against the government. It gives the responsibility to every citizen of this great nation to obey the mandate of Congress and the lawful orders of the President in order to protect and preserve and build this nation, to give one's very life for our nation. These are broad powers and responsibilities, but there are indeed limits to their scope.

In Article 1, Section 8, the Constitution also clearly gives Congress the power and responsibility to declare war, when that sad but terrible occasion might present itself.

We can read from the Federalist Papers by Hamilton, Madison, and John Jay, in which they examine the powers of the President and Congress and compare the President's powers with that of the British King. Hamilton herein points out that the

> President is to be Commander-in-Chief of the Army and Navy of the United States. In this respect his authority would be nominally the same with that of the King of Great Britain, but in substance much inferior to it. It would amount to nothing more than the command and direction of the military and naval forces ... while that of the British King extends to the *declaring* of war and to the *raising* and *regulating* of fleets and armies, all of which by the Constitution under consideration would appertain to the legislature. (emphasis Hamilton's.)

Later Hamilton repeats the difference between the President on the one hand and the King of England on the other. "The one (the President) would have a right to command the military and naval forces of the nation; the other (the King) in addition to this right, possesses that of *declaring* war, and of *raising* and *regulating* fleets and armies by his own authority."

For over a decade we have been engaged in a great and dangerous war. Forty thousand American soldiers have been killed. It is estimated that if the war were to end today, the total cost of the war including pensions and other benefits yet to be paid, would cost $350 billion. Our young men and women of this nation, and many citizens mature in age, abhor this war and question the initial judgment that has led to this war. Many who wish to remain in Vietnam do so because they say our good name is involved, but that we should never have been there in the first place. This is a shaky basis upon which to lead men to battle and our nation to war.

There are some citizens who have questioned the President's constitutional authority to continue to conduct this war. They say: "No war has been declared by Congress" as the Constitution provides;

142

that under these circumstances, the President, however well-meaning, however sincere his actions and motivations, is exceeding his power under the Constitution. They say the Tonkin Gulf Resolution of 1964 is not a declaration of war and if this be the authority for conducting the war, the Resolution as acted upon by the President is an unconstitutional delegation of power by the two branches of government acting together.

The proposed Massachusetts statute does not, however, make this determination. This statute changes no law, attempts to curtail no power of Congress, of the President, or of the Army or the Navy guaranteed or authorized by the Constitution. It seeks to have a judicial determination by the United States Supreme Court as to the scope and the breadth of the presidential and congressional powers. It seeks to restore a government of law and not of men. For we live under a government that insures and guarantees in writing the fact that there shall not be untrammeled dictatorial power by any branch or even two branches of our government acting in sincere but terrible ignorance of their powers and responsibilities.

What this Bill does do is seek by our constitutional, judicial process a judicial determination of whether the President or Congress are acting beyond their powers, because no war has been declared. Under this Bill the Commonwealth of Massachusetts mandates our chief lawyer, the attorney general, the lawyer for the people, to join in a judicial inquiry before the United States Supreme Court in the great constitutional tradition of our nation to determine the limits to the war-making authority of our executive and legislative branches of government.

Today, our youth are crying out against a society that they see is unable to solve its problems of racial animosity, housing, pollution of the air we breathe, welfare, medical care; a nation engaged in a vast, seemingly endless war in Laos, Cambodia, Vietnam, perhaps Thailand and the whole vast area of Indo-China, against a peasant people that we little know and whom we really intended to help. In helping these people, we have caused death and destruction to perhaps a half million of a 35-million population.

Our youth are crying out to us to take steps to bring about an end to the war and solve our internal problems. They cry out in deep and bitter despair against an affluent society that cannot bring inner peace to its citizens.

Hopefully we can bring about a speedy end to this war without internal violence so that we might go about the business of re-structuring and remodeling our society to meet the challenges of today.

22 The Battle of the Leaflets

Fred King

I have been deeply disturbed by the deterioration of our constitutional democracy and its replacement by "executive order." What is even more alarming is the acceptance of this political phenomenon by a large number of Americans. The way people have been "Madison Avenued" into believing in a leader, and not having self-confidence in their own ability to participate in the decision-making process, is frightening. There are many reasons for people's accepting authoritarian decisions handed down to them from above. Perhaps the chief one is that they believe that the President has available to him some secret information that cannot be made known to the public for fear that the "enemy" will find out he knows something that they think he does not know.

It is easy to give the public a snow job on what's going on in Southeast Asia, since most people know very little about the area and its political, military, and economic complexities. But almost everybody knows that the Constitution of the United States give Congress the power to declare war and that Congress has not declared war—and maybe there is something wrong with fighting a war for "freedom" when at the same time our freedoms, guaranteed by the Constitution, are denied our own citizens.

When I first heard of the Shea-Wells Bill I decided to support it with all I had. Even if it did not become law, it would point out to the American people the meaning of the Constitution and what the war was

145

doing to it. I knew that by relating the peace issue to the Constitution it would be possible to broaden the base of opposition to the war. I went to the press conference on January 26, 1970 and was extemely impressed by Rep. Jim Shea, Rev. John Wells and Prof. Steve Worth. I did not know John or Steve, and had worked only a little with Jim Shea after I coordinated the signature drive for Gene McCarthy in Newton. I gathered all the material given out at the press conference. Being the chairman of the Newton Moratorium Committee for the month of January, I called a meeting for January 28 to organize support for the Bill.

The meeting was at the home of Sev and Louise Bruyn who had been Moratorium leaders in October. It was a very successful meeting; Cathy Knight assumed most of the responsibilities and really carried through. I was not unsuccessful in my attempt to convince the group to put out a leaflet. In the middle of winter, leaflet-distribution was a problem, especially for a cause that we were afraid didn't have a chance in hell of succeeding. Publicity for the public hearing was an even more serious problem. Lack of money made it impossible to advertise on radio, TV, or in newspapers. I was still convinced that concentrated leafleting was necessary for a large turnout at the public hearing, and no matter how good a case the scholars presented to the Judiciary Committee, popular support for the Bill had to be proven.

On Thursday, January 27, I called Rev. John Wells, who was out of town, but Mrs. Wells referred me to Mrs. Mary Ann Seitz. When I called Mary Ann, she invited me to the Lexington meeting scheduled for the next day, Friday, January 30. At the meeting I again volunteered to write a leaflet and, subject to the group's approval, take it to the printer and organize a state-wide distribution campaign. It was too late to get the Bill endorsed by various organizations, so instead I requested that they act as information centers and allow their names, addresses, and telephone numbers to be listed on the leaflet. Everything went smoothly over the weekend. Jim, John, and Steve liked the leaflet so I went to the printer on Monday, February 2, and twenty thousand were ready for distribution February 4. I told some employees at the press that this was the most important thing that they had ever printed. They were bearish; they said that they had printed many other leaflets against the Vietnam war and were not really convinced that this was significantly different.

On the evening of February 4, the Newton Coalition for New Politics sponsored a meeting at the Grace Episcopal Church. The featured speakers were Father Robert Drinan, candidate for Congress, and Bill Strong, who reported on his visit to Cuba. I placed a leaflet on every empty chair before people arrived and later gave a brief report on the Bill, urging people to take leaflets on their way out and to come to the public hearing on February 11.

After my report I went to the literature table to hand out bundles of leaflets to people as they came in and out of the meeting. It was very surprising to find out how many people had forgotten about the announcement of the public meeting for Feburary 11—and this should be a good lesson to organizers. *Announcements have very little effect without a follow-up.* Fortunately, the formal part of the meeting ended early and many people stayed and chatted for more than another half hour, which gave me time to move out five thousand leaflets. I distributed bundles of one hundred to five hundred to Brookline PAX; through Elmer and Alice Fehlhauber I gave out one thousand; and five hundred went to Simmons College via Mark Solomon. Bundles were also routed to Brandeis University, Northeastern University, Tufts University, M.I.T., Boston College, Boston University, Newton High School, Newton South High, and many churches.

The very next day, Thursday, February 5, I called the printer and ordered another twenty thousand copies and told Bob Harwich of Harwich Lithograph to change Room 122 in the copy to Gardner Auditorium. Room 122 was rather small, and it was my understanding that the Judiciary Committee had made tentative arrangements to use Gardner Auditorium if there were a large enough turnout. The *Boston Globe* estimated eight hundred attended the hearing, but my guess was that this was the peak; during the afternoon and evening many left and new people came. Undoubtedly there were well over a thousand.

Toward the latter part of the meeting, the Chairman of the Judiciary Committee, Joe Ward, asked the audience how many were in favor of the Bill. Almost everyone put up his hand. Only one person, Reverend Bates, raised his hand when it was asked who was opposed. I said jokingly to Steve Worth's secretary, "He may go down in history as the man who killed the Bill."

The next day, Thursday, February 12, we had a little victory party in Lexington and decided to produce a third edition of the leaflets. This time the names, addresses, and telephone numbers, both at home and in the State House, of all members of the Judiciary Committee were listed on the leaflet. Thirty thousand copies were distributed state-wide, with colleges, high schools, churches, and peace organizations the primary distributors. Numerous letters, telegrams, and telephone calls were received by members of the Judiciary Committee after the February 11 hearing and right up to the time that the Bill was reported out of committee with a favorable recommendation.

Notwithstanding the remarkable success of the public hearing—as Chairman Joseph Ward put it "the most impressive he had seen during his twenty years as a legislator"—there was little coverage nationally.

Quite often peculiar little court cases on a local level reach the national media, but why this important Bill failed to do so is still a mystery to me. I wondered at the time if this was a result of Spiro Agnew's intimidation of the news media. Since we were so successful in the peace effort by linking peace with the United States Constitution, I decided at noon on Friday, the thirteenth, to go to the New Democratic Coalition Convention in Chicago that weekend. Reverend Duggan at the PAX office said John Elder, chairman of Citizens for Participation Politics (C.P.P.) and Al Levin were leaving on the 3 o'clock plane. I called home to tell my wife that I was joining them and armed with two thousand leaflets, and my tooth brush, I headed for Logan Airport and bumped into John Elder in the subway; we met Al on the plane. We met the rest of our delegation, Dick Cauchi, Jim Murphy, Bob Kavin, E. J. Dionne, Dave Williams, Lenny Jones, and Claudis Morrer in Chicago.

Friday was not productive, but on Saturday there was considerable opportunity to talk with small groups of people about the Bill. Unfortunately, I left for Chicago in such a hurry that I did not have all the material written by Wells, Shea, and Worth, but managed to answer the questions from the floor well enough to convince the delegates that this was not Southern interposition and that if the war were unconstitutional, then it is a violation of an individual's constitutional rights to force him to fight in such a war. Further, I pointed out it is the responsibility of all elected officials to defend the constitutional rights of the people they represent, especially if Congress fails to assume its responsibility. I also emphasized that the momentum from this campaign for the Shea-Wells Bill in Massachusetts could crescendo to the national level. Many people in Congress are anxious to do a good job on the peace issue, but don't always have the courage of their convictions. But this kind of legislation has popular appeal and stops the opposition cold, and politicians feel comfortable with it.

One question that was quite amusing was, "Do you seriously think the state of Massachusetts will enact this Bill into law?" My answer was,

"Let me put it this way—our public hearing was a smashing success and the campaign was picking up considerable momentum. I have had quite a bit of political experience and never saw anything that caught on like this. I highly recommend that you introduce similar Bills in your home states. Even if you are not successful in getting the Bills passed, you will develop an organization that will be productive in other areas. You will also prove to the politicians that people support this kind of legislation and want their constitutional rights protected. In so doing, it will encourage senators and congressmen to speak out against unconstitutional exercise of federal power. Our efforts will eventually lead to federal laws or amendments to the Constitution that will protect the American people from getting into wars by executive order."

I was afraid of being too optimistic and conveying the impression that success depended only upon the passage of the Bill. I *was* optimistic—and also confident that the thirty thousand new leaflets coming out with the names, addresses, and telephone numbers of the Judiciary Committee members would result in their receiving letters, telegrams, and phone calls supporting the Bill, and that this could result in their reporting it out favorably. I also knew that the word would get out to the other legislators that the Judiciary Committee members were getting favorable support from the voters.

The Shea-Wells Bill got the endorsement of the convention and two thousand copies of the Bill got into the hands of key people in twenty-seven other states. When this got back to Massachusetts it sparked more enthusiasm among our supporters to know that groups in other states were carrying on similar efforts.

From February 28 to March 1 there was a Peace Conference at M.I.T. We set up a table and got quite a mixed reaction. It was strikingly apparent that the Right did not have a monopoly on the lunatics. Many leftists would not support the Bill because it was working within the system. Others opposed it because it would not completely smash the "monopolistic, military industrial structure that was the cause of the war."

I called Howard Zinn and told him of the opposition to the Shea Bill by some radicals who opposed the war, and I urged him to do what he could to ward off this damaging influence. He agreed that "the war had to be opposed on all levels" and the Shea Bill, even though it would not stop the war, was certainly a step in the right direction. Later, he told me that there was no real need to counteract the influence of this ultra-left that I met at the conference, and that most of his associates

149

supported the Shea Bill however much they might have differed as to its effectiveness.

There is a lesson that must be learned from this, especially for young activists, namely, that there are a lot of kooky people who get involved in good causes and do more harm than good. We must not allow ourselves to get bogged down by their actions.

On March 7 there was an eclipse of the sun in the Boston area, and it seemed to me that we would be able to put the eclipse to work for us too. Knowing that people would be looking at the sky as it darkened, I thought it would be a good idea to send an airplane up to write H2396. I called John Wells and he found a sky writer and made arrangements within ten minutes. We alerted the news media and people called the talk shows to tell them why the airplane was writing H2396 in the sky. The campaign was so exciting that I thought we would write a book about it someday and this would make a good picture for the book. It gave us some more publicity and to my knowledge it was the only time that this had been done.

It may come as a surprise to many, but it is very doubtful that any meeting took place at Harvard University to support this Bill. Yet ten thousand copies of the leaflets moved out from Harvard. From my physics labs the students brought leaflets to every dormitory and dining hall on the campus. Teachers taking my evening course in physics carried hundreds of leaflets to their high schools. Adjacent to our labs is the Harvard Graduate School of Education, and many of its teachers brought leaflets to schools with which they were affiliated. There is little wonder that many legislators reported getting calls from constitutents they never heard of before.

As the time approached for the Bill to be voted on by the legislature, Mary Strauss, Stillman and Elizabeth Williams, and I compiled the names, addresses, and telephone numbers of all the state representatives and senators and organized them along congressional district lines.

This may sound strange, but with congressional campaigns in the making this year, I thought that the Shea-Wells Bill could help strengthen congressional organizations so that even if the Bill were defeated, the campaign for it would help build grass roots strength for the Fall elections. This is a pretty simple idea and is certainly not new, but it was amazing to find so many people whose hearts are in the right place, but who did not understand this strategy in practical terms. Since the constitutionality of the Bill was questionable, some were hesitant to put much effort into supporting it. I myself was not absolutely sure about its constitutional validity in January; but I still supported it because in spite of any imperfections, it focussed on the possible unconstitutionality of the war and I felt any worthwhile effort in this respect might lead to something more productive later. The "fringe benefits" were too tempting to pass up.

I hope that others will learn from this experience and not get stifled by technicalities. You have to keep in mind the main objective. There will always be those who can present excellent reasons as to why something will fail. They were the biggest problem. If the Bill had failed to pass, it would not have been due to the opposition from the Right—it would have been from the "confusers" in the peace movement.

Of course it might be said that the Supreme Court has not acted on a test case yet. True, but the Shea-Wells Bill has already accomplished exactly what I wanted it to do, regardless of what happens in the courts. It has forced the Congress of the United States to take steps to get its house in constitutional order. I have no doubt that Nixon's invasion of Cambodia would have been challenged by the Senate and on constitutional grounds without the Shea-Wells law, but not with the same order of magnitude.

I am very confident that the enactment of the Shea-Wells law has opened a new era in American politics, and I am convinced that new regulations limiting the power of the President to commit American men to combat will be forthcoming. I am hopeful that eventually we will see an amendment to the United States Constitution that will require more than a simple majority vote to declare war; maybe four fifths or nine tenths would be appropriate. Perhaps it would even be wise to require Congress to vote to sustain a declaration of war periodically; failure to sustain the declaration would require the withdrawal of all American forces within thirty days. Another possibility to think about is that we may not declare war on anyone unless the United States is attacked directly, and that if we are to engage in a "police action," no more than 10 per cent of the troops involved shall be Americans. The Constitution should also state specifically that under no circumstances whatsoever shall the President or the Congress have the power to cancel any future election.

23   Getting to the People

David Lustig

When I first heard about the Massachusetts Vietnam Bill I was a graduate student at Northeastern University in Boston. I was taking a seminar in civil rights from Prof. Steve Worth, who had been an instructor of mine since my undergraduate days at Northeastern. Just before class one day Professor Worth told me he was working on a piece of legislation that had been introduced in the Massachusetts Legislature, to put the Vietnam war to a constitutional test.

My immediate reaction was one of skepticism. I considered the chances less than nil that a piece of state legislation would achieve a United States Supreme Court test. And having some knowledge of Massachusetts politics, I considered the chances of even as dove-ish a state as Massachusetts' passing an act like this to be approximately nil, too. But in the end I was impressed by his arguments, and when Professor Worth asked if I would set up a press conference to explain the proposed legislation I agreed. Worth explained that the original Bill had been drawn up by Rev. John Wells of the First Parish Unitarian Church in Lexington, Massachusetts. We then arranged to have a meeting at Representative Shea's office in the State House. Present at the meeting were Worth, Shea, Mary Ann Seitz, John Wells, Dick Cauchi (Executive Secretary, Citizens for Participation Politics), and Jane Webb. Jane was at that time executive secretary of Mass. PAX, which is chaired by Jerry Grossman, president of Massachusetts Envelope Company. Also there were John Businger, a student at Boston College Law School and an assistant to Shea, and Ron Rosenblith, who had been working on youth affairs.

We set a time for the press conference, 10:30 a.m. Monday morning, January 26, 1970, to be held in Room 443, directly across from Shea's office. Room 443 is a hearing room that can accommodate about fifteen to twenty people around a large table and that has space for about forty to fifty people in the gallery. We agreed this gallery space should be occupied by high school students and draft-age kids from Lexington.

I contacted approximately twenty-five to thirty radio and television stations, and magazines and newspapers in the Boston area. I did not expect the initial reaction to be favorable, considering that we were dealing with rather a novel piece of legislation, and that Bills challenging the war were usually considered by the press as an attempt by the sponsors to gain some sort of political leverage. The reaction was as bad as I expected it to be. We had people from the State House news service, one reporter from the *Boston Globe,* a camera crew from WBZ-TV (NBC's local station), and one man from Boston's Channel 56, an independent television station. Also present were assorted members of the college press.

Before the press conference, and at it as well, we had distributed a number of releases and statements explaining the Bill, which was at that time known as H 2396. The first of these was an endorsement by prominent groups and citizens, including the National Mobilization Committee to end the War in Vietnam; Mass. PAX; Rep. William Fitz Ryan, D., of New York City; former Sen. Joseph Clark, D., Penn.; and three constitutional law experts, Allen Dershowitz of Harvard, Warren Schwartz of the University of Illinois, and Lawrence Velvel from the University of Kansas. A few days later we issued another release with endorsements from former Sen. Ernest G. Gruening, D., Alaska, who was one of two Senators (Wayne Morse was the other) to vote against the Tonkin Gulf Resolution in 1964 and Dr. Benjamin Spock. Spock's statement read:

> House Bill 2396 provides a legal remedy to a very human problem, the problem that every young man faces when he is told by his government that he must fight in a war which he believes to be illegal and knows to be immoral . . . The war is illegal for many reasons, but first because Congress has never declared it. If you pass this Bill the authority of the Commonwealth will be brought to bear on the side of legality as well as on

the side of morality. I sincerely hope that you will enact this proposal and that other states throughout the country will take similar action.

After the press conference a couple of things were immediately clear to me. In the first place this piece of legislation, if it was to pass, was going to pass primarily because of Representative Shea's actions in the State House, and because of his association with House Speaker David Bartley and Senate Pres. Maurice Donahue. It was therefore, from a political public relations standpoint, imperative that the public identify the Bill with Representative Shea. After all he was the legislator who was going to be involved in floor fights on the Bill, not Reverend Wells or Professor Worth. A second thing that occurred to me was that we had to reach two basic audiences. One, the highly politicized, was relatively easy to reach and to convince. This group included people aligned with either CPP or Mass. PAX, or with any of the myriad peace organizations. I felt television appeals to them were fairly unnecessary, since they were already "in the bag," as it were. But the second audience, the non-politically inclined, was the tough nut we had to crack; and these people were generally unresponsive to political television appeals.

During my stint producing the Jerry Williams radio talk show in Boston, I had done considerable research on its audience, which Jerry once said was typified by a fellow from South Boston who comes home at night from his blue-collar job, takes off his shoes, puts his feet up on a table, and grabs a six-pack of beer. It was this type of person we wanted to reach. So immediately after we finished the press conference I started making contact with the most popular talk masters in the city. Meanwhile I was working on getting the press to the Judiciary Committee hearing set for February 11, at which nationally known constitutional experts were to testify. A week before the meeting I sent out a press release, which I followed up the next day with phone calls. Then I sent out a second press notice on Representative Shea's stationery, and finally two days before the hearing I again called the various news editors. We had, I would estimate, between forty and fifty representatives of news media at the hearing on February 11, including all the major radio and television stations in Boston. I had called news editors in New York City at NBC, CBS, and ABC; this prompted them to request footage from their local outlets, for possible national transmission.

My contacts with the talk shows were also paying off. The night before the hearing, the evening of the tenth, we appeared on Jerry

155

Williams's program for an hour and a half. Included on that program were attorney Larry Velvel from the University of Kansas and attorney Michael Tigar from UCLA Law School, both constitutional experts who had flown to Boston for the hearing the following day. The Monday before, February ninth, from 10 until 2 in the morning we appeared on Steve Frederick's show and on the morning of the tenth we appeared on the "New England Today" program.

I believe the impact of the talk programs was decisive, absolutely decisive, in creating a favorable public atmosphere at the hearing on February 11. The room overflowed with Gold Star Mothers, Vietnam veterans of all shades and descriptions, blacks, whites, the young and not so young, old people with canes, people in wheel chairs, blind people with seeing-eye dogs. From a random sampling I learned that the presence of the older people, at least, was directly attributable to talk programs we participated in the three or four days before the hearing.

I think we made three points clear to the voters and to the legislators. We brought home to them that the belief in constitutional thinking was a deeply rooted tradition in the people of Massachusetts. Secondly, we made it clear that Massachusetts and its citizens also expected the federal government to respect the Constitution and its laws. And thirdly, we tried to emphasize that our attack was not directed at the Vietnam war, but at whether or not it was a *legally declared* war.

In all my work with the public on behalf of the Shea Bill I thought it was important to cultivate the idea that we were opposed to an unconstitutional exercise of power by the executive department on *any* sort of military situation. The Dominican Republic and Korea, for example, were two other areas in which many of us felt the President acted illegally. I think this stand attracted the support of certain conservatives who like to call themselves, along with President Nixon and Vice President Agnew, "strict constructionists."

Following the hearing on February 11, our first effort, after we relaxed a bit from two weeks of intensive strain, was to redraft the Bill, which obviously had several problems. In the first place, Section 1 of the original version required that the Bill would take effect only after sixty days from the initiation of hostilities; this was dropped. Wells worked long hours on the rewording, together with William Homans, a Boston lawyer, and others. It became obvious more time was needed, since everyone involved had his regular day-to-day work to pursue, and we were gratified indeed when Senator Ward several times extended our

156

deadline, which we felt was a recognition of the worth of our Bill. Meanwhile, our lobbying efforts continued. The groups and people committed to our cause held rallies in various towns and at our request kept up a campaign of letters and phone calls to the key members of the Judiciary Committee and to people who lived in their areas. Representative Martin Linsky, a Republican who voted in favor of the Bill, told me he thought it was one of the most effective and high-caliber lobbying jobs he had ever observed.

Finally it was determined that the Bill would be presented at an Executive Hearing on the morning of Tuesday, March 10, so we scheduled a press conference for the next morning, in the Judiciary Committee hearing room, Room 222 at the State House. At this point the Bill had been sent on to the Ways and Means Committee—we did not learn until 3:00 p.m. that day that the legislation had been favorably reported to go to the floor of the House and that House Speaker David Bartley would speak on its behalf. His support was both significant and essential, and we were elated. The House was much more split than the Senate on the issue of peace; we knew from the outset that we did not have the kind of support in the House that we desperately needed.

At the Press Conference we made as much as we could of the fact that the Judiciary Committee in Executive session had given its unanimous approval to the Bill. There are twenty-one members on the Committee. The vote was 11-0; some did not show up for the meeting and a few simply did not vote.

On Thursday, the twelfth, the Bill (now known as H 5165) went to the House. The gallery was packed, and even the Speaker's gallery had been opened to the overflow crowd. The place was swarming with TV and newsmen. The debate has been fully covered elsewhere in this book, but I would like to stress again it was clearly evident that the argument having the most impact was that the legislation was trying to reaffirm for soldiers what has always been a right for all citizens—the right to sue in the Courts for one's constitutional rights and prerogatives. This had never been a problem in domestic issues; now we were bringing in foreign policy, but still basically the issue was a citizen's rights.

The vote passed the House 116-110 by a margin of six votes, and on Monday, the sixteenth, the House would meet again for a second reading and vote, leaving opponents three days to change the votes of three people for a tie vote; four votes had to be changed to defeat the legislation. We were in a bad position, to put it mildly. Among other problems veterans' groups, who opposed the Bill but assumed it would be defeated and so had not worked against it, now spent an active weekend lobbying. The Speaker himself was in a bad position, since his authority as a speaker and a politician would be seriously affected by defeat of the Bill.

The first thing we did was to send out a press release thanking Speaker Bartley for his support of the Bill on the floor. We also issued another release reaffirming our faith in working through the system to ensure constitutional rights. And finally we sent out a third statement aimed at clarifying any remaining doubts about the legal validity of this approach to test whether or not an undeclared war is constitutional. I believe this last release had a great deal of influence on those who were undecided. On Friday, the thirteenth, we received a telegram of support from Dr. Richard Falk, an international law expert from Princeton, which we promptly sent to Bartley, Sargent, and others. Meanwhile we urged all the groups with us to intensify their phoning campaign, even though it was a weekend.

All weekend we had been concerned about rumors that the veterans were going to lobby in force against the Bill. I must point out one thing; we put the veterans in a very difficult position because our Bill was put forth on the floor of the House as a bill to aid veterans, since it hoped to guarantee servicemen a right we believed they had under the Constitution. Therefore, it was very difficult for veterans to go out and argue against a Bill like this. As it turned out, on Monday we lost only one vote from the pressure of the veterans' group. That morning we got a formal endorsement from Mayor White, almost too late for it to do any good, although the Mayor did do some lobbying with representatives in the House in favor of the Bill.

The vote of Monday, and Governor Sargent's signature, is now history. I think we accomplished three things: First, we reopened the debate on the war at a time when people were bogging down in apathy; second, we proved that the "silent majority" was by no means all for Nixon's doctrines; and third—and most important—we proved the system works. Other states have taken up our cause, and the case now rests with the Supreme Court where we hope Jim Shea's faith will be vindicated.

158

24   In the House of Representatives

David M. Bartley

As the chief presiding officer of the Massachusetts House of Representatives, the Speaker of the House very rarely lends the prestige of his office to either side when legislative proposals are being debated before the membership.

Yet, in the spring of 1970, I left my rostrum twice within a period of a little more than two weeks, to personally join in debating two very different, yet very related issues.

The first issue was big news in Massachusetts. The second has become big news nationally and internationally.

The two issues—and their relationship one to another—were spelled out in my speech to the House on the afternoon of March 12, 1970 (See Chapter 3 for text of speech).

My fight of two weeks earlier was aimed at preventing a 33 per cent reduction in the membership of the Massachusetts House of Representatives. I felt the reduction would further strengthen the already strong office of governor. And I feared that this increased executive power would come at the expense of the House traditionally a closer-to-the-people or "populist" branch.

I won my fight against the House-cut amendment even though the backers of the House-cut amendment (including, naturally, the state's chief executive), needed just 70 of 280 votes to carry the motion. They got 69, I got 191, a one-vote margin of victory.

When I took to the floor to debate the Shea Bill, I felt the margin could be equally as close, perhaps a two- or three-vote edge.

We won by six.

My first acquaintance with the Shea Bill came in January, 1970, when Rep. Jim Shea and I talked over the general philosophy behind the legislation. At that point in time, I did not hold out great hopes for the passage of the legislation. As a non-lawyer, I was unsure of the legal footing of the proposal. As a legislative leader, I could visualize the roar of "guffaws" from much of the press if the Massachusetts Legislature "started tinkering with foreign policy."

But as a politician, with reasonably sensitive political antennae, I was aware that a large segment of Massachusetts society was fed up with the continued waging of an open-ended war. The potential of public support for such revolutionary legislation as the Shea Bill was there. And if that support could be focussed on any body of men or institution of government, it could be most easily focussed on the men serving as state representatives in our relatively small, compact, and close-to-the-grass-roots state representative districts.

Additionally, I saw the Shea Bill as offering a positive opportunity for a state Legislature to address itself to the important question of executive usurpation of legislative prerogatives.

At the same time I fully realized that no piece of state legislation could ever replace the American, Vietnamese, and now Cambodian lives lost in the Southeast Asian war. Nor would a single piece of state legislation bind the physical injuries and heal the psychological wounds of the victims of that war. Nor would it stop the spiral of arms spending. Nor would it, of itself, help free the money needed to build the housing, feed the hungry, or end discrimination around the world.

But the Bill did offer this. It did offer an opportunity for a duly elected body of government to raise its voice over an issue that was gnawing at the fabric of American society, that was dividing America against herself. It did offer the opportunity of peaceful parliamentary protest by elected representatives of the people. And that message could not be ignored.

On February 11, the Shea Bill was scheduled for a public hearing before the Joint Legislative Committee on the Judiciary. This hearing would probe the legal ramifications of the legislation, taking testimony from parties both for and against the proposal. On the eve of the hearing I still had doubts about the Bill's chance of passage, regardless of its merit.

But the hearing was an eye-opener. Some eight hundred people crowded into the auditorium, almost all of them favoring the measure. Importantly, testimony was to the point. Some legislators had feared that an outpouring of the "kook element" would "turn-off" those who might otherwise vote for the Bill. The "kooks" weren't there. But legal and constitutional experts were. And so were hundreds of citizens, young and middle-aged and old, long hairs and short hairs—all seriously concerned over the war, and what effect this legislation might have in speeding up the conclusion of those hostilities.

I began to feel then that the Shea Bill had begun to move, that it was being called forward by the quiet hand of Thoreau's distant drummer.

Legislative reporters, legislative observers, and legislators themselves, impressed with the demeanor of the hearing, also began to feel that the Bill was moving, that there was serious interest in it, that there was serious support for it.

Following the hearing, members of my staff including Timothy J. Taylor, press secretary, and John T. Eller, legislative assistant, met with Representative Shea, John Businger (Rep. Shea's assistant), Senate Pres. Maurice A. Donahue and his staff, Rev. John Wells, Prof. Steve Worth, Ronald Rosenblith, and people from Massachusetts PAX, Citizens for Participation Politics, and many other concerned groups.

Aware of my support of the legislation, my staff urged active participation in seeking the votes necessary to secure passage of the Bill. They were aware of the up-hill fight that would have to be waged to win the battle. We were still recovering from the exhausting months of struggle to win the House-cut fight. But all agreed that a similar effort would be made on behalf of the Shea Bill—"If."

And that "If" was simply this. If the Joint Legislative Committee on the Judiciary found the Bill legally, legislatively, and constitutionally feasible and realistic, we would join the battle.

John Eller submitted the following (condensed) summary to me on the Shea Bill, as it stood following a preliminary redrafting by the Judiciary Committee:

Summary Statement for Support of House Bill 5165 (Memorandum to House Speaker David M. Bartley, March 10, 1970)

Public Support
800 people appeared in favor of this Bill at public hearing. Rep. Dan Carney said it was the most significant public hearing in years. These people were seeking a way to register their anguish that over 40,000 American boys have been killed and 220,000 wounded in a congressionally undeclared war.

Tradition

Major changes in American life have begun in Massachusetts. The Revolution itself began here as did the Abolitionist Movement, the Mexican American War peace movement. This stands us well beside early reformers.

Constitutionality

H. 5165 is a strict constructionist Bill requiring a court determination whether the President has usurped congressional powers to declare war guaranteed by the U.S. Constitution (1:8). The Bill does not question treaties or congressionally approved conscription. It only asks the Supreme Court to determine if Congress's war-declaring power has been usurped, and if so it seeks to return certain national constitutional power to the people's national legislators.

Role of Legislature

Reformers have canonized creative executive power and lauded its extension on all levels. This extension has resulted in loss of legislative power on each level. This Bill reasserts state legislative power to insist on a Supreme Court decision to either affirm or deny the war-making power of Congress.

Role of Attorney General

The reasons that this Bill involves the executive machinery of the Commonwealth (the attorney general) are three:

1. The impact of the judicial process of a state action is by its effect a class action and, thus, diminishes the possibility of a series of private initiatives to establish the enforcement of the right which this law will establish.

2. This law will partially remove the financial burden from an individual.

3. This Bill as a law will maximize the chances for a still-remote Supreme Court ruling.

I spoke with and received affirmative responses on the value of the Bill from Judiciary Committee Chairmen Representative Cornelius Kiernan (D-Lowell) and Sen. Joseph D. Ward (D-Fitchburg). I spoke with the attorney general, Robert H. Quinn, and solicited his views regarding the proposal. He felt the Bill was reasonable and timely. In addition I spoke at length with Senate Pres. Maurice A. Donahue and commended him for his courageous and early support of the basic concepts of this Bill. I then met with the Judiciary Committee late in the afternoon as it held its final executive session on the Bill and indicated my support of the Bill to the Committee as they completed the final draft. The Committee members had satisfied themselves as to the constitutional merit of the Bill and later that day reported favorably the redrafted version, which was immediately printed. We then proceeded to establish the timetable for the Bill and scheduled the House debate for March 12, 1970. We were in the fight.

On March 10-11 my staff and I discussed the upcoming debate. One administrative assistant urged that the House amend the Bill to make its provisions effective only if approved by the voters in the November, 1970 election. He felt confident that the Shea Bill would be passed by the Legislature and that it would win approval if submitted to the voters. His argument was that Legislative approval of this measure coupled with a follow-up endorsement of the Bill at the polls would be an even more forceful indication to the national administration of the people's concern over the constitutionality of the Vietnam war.

Others on the staff felt that certain segments of the press might interpret such action as a "cop-out"—that the Legislature didn't want to make the final decision itself on such a controversial and unprecedented piece of legislation. Opponents of the referendum amendment in this discussion agreed that an affirmative legislative vote, coupled with a follow-up vote of approval in November, would give the Shea legislation more impact. But they debated and won the point that many of the major daily newspapers in the Commonwealth (with the exception of the *Boston Globe*) mocked and ridiculed the Shea Bill and would use the referendum amendment to question the sincerity of the Legislature, and the sincerity of the Shea Bill itself.

The decision was made *not* to add a referendum amendment to the Shea Bill for fear it might jeopardize its passage.

Interestingly enough, two weeks later, student leaders on both the state and national level began a major campaign for a Vietnam war referendum in the various states.

(The Vietnam war referendum, which we decided to forego in the name of realistic political compromise, has since come to pass, though not on the Shea Bill itself. A War Referendum question, filed by Senate Pres. Maurice A. Donahue (D-Holyoke) was passed by the Legislature and signed into law in July, 1970 for placement on the November, 1970 Massachusetts state ballot.)

On March 12 the issue came to the floor of the House for debate. Members of my staff met with various legislators to explain the reasonableness of the Bill and ask their support.

There was a profound sense of historical significance in the House chamber that day as debate began. There were also deep emotional feelings on both sides of the issue. The debate in the House was long, generally eloquent, and moving. There were warnings that passage of the Bill would constitute "aid and comfort for Hanoi"; that backers of the Bill were in league with "Godless Communism" and with the "Communist regime." The speakers were sincere. Their support of the Bill, or their opposition, their hopes or their fears and frustrations were, in fact, a microcosm of the nation's feelings over Vietnam.

163

And, although the Shea Bill generated both bipartisan support and opposition, there was politics.

Democratic supporters of the Bill realized that were the measure passed and sent to the governor, a Republican, he would be forced to break his careful silence on the measure and either approve it (and thus follow the lead of the Democratic legislative leadership) or veto it (and incur the wrath of the decidedly anti-Nixon Massachusetts electorate who would regard the action as an endorsement of Nixon's war position).

Republicans opposed to the Bill thought their governor ought to be spared having to make such a choice.

It must be pointed out in fairness to all concerned that the merit of the Bill, or the lack of merit, and the politics of its passage or of its defeat were not automatically exclusive motives. And I am not aware of any great number of legislators of either party who finally voted for or against the Bill for strictly political reasons, though I am sure that it would be reasonable to assume that there were such votes cast on both sides.

Members of the governor's staff, however, were working the corridors outside the House chamber as debate went on. The governor's Legal Counsel had appeared before a Republican caucus earlier in the day and reportedly urged that amendments be added to the Bill to divert it from the governor's desk. The Republican chief executive (despite the reported urgings of some liberals on his staff) was not anxious to see the Bill land on his desk and force a decision that might result in some discomfort for the Nixon-Agnew Administration. Publicly, the Republican governor maintained a studied pose of ambiguity.

The first key test of the Bill came when the House Republican leadership proposed, as had been suggested by the governor's lieutenants at the GOP caucus, that the Shea Bill be referred to the Democratic attorney general of Massachusetts for a ruling on its constitutionality. That move was rejected 54 to 173, with 153 Democrats and 20 Republicans joining forces to keep the Bill alive.

Shifting the Bill to the attorney general would have accomplished one major political end, the governor's people argued privately. It would have forced the Democratic attorney general to make the first, critical public decision. If he approved the Bill, the governor could then approve it, shrug his shoulders, and say, "the (Democratic) attorney general said it was OK." On the other hand, if the attorney general ruled against the legislation, the governor could say, "the (Democratic) attorney general has said it's unconstitutional, I can't support it."

It was a classic political dodge. But it was easily seen through. On this particular roll call more than any other, Democrats who might have opposed the Bill gave it a vote of support in order to force the Republican governor to make a decision on it, and Republicans who might have supported the Bill voted to sidetrack it to protect their governor from a hot issue. If the final vote was an ideological roll call, this vote was the roll call on the politics of the Shea Bill.

A second move was made to kill the Bill outright by referring it to the "next annual session" of the Legislature.

This was the key roll call. It followed three and one-half hours of debate, during which time I managed to break one gavel in pounding the chamber into order.

As I switched on the electric roll-call machine for the vote, I couldn't help thinking that this roll call was of truly historic dimensions. I recalled the eloquent defense of the Bill on the floor of the House by Representative Kiernan, the Judiciary Committee chairman.

He pointed out that he (as I) had had early reservations as to the constitutionality of the Bill before us. But after weeks of study, he became convinced of the Bill's merit. His research, he said, indicated no legal or constitutional precedent whereby a citizen who felt himself aggrieved by his government's policy could not seek an adjudication of his complaint in the courts. Yet, in precisely the area before us, the constitutional requirement that the President receive from Congress a formal declaration of war prior to committing American men to a foreign conflict, there existed no such legal vehicle to obtain such adjudication. This situation, he said, was intolerable. For it left a vacuum in the process of constitutional government that was rapidly being exploited by radicals who, in the name of peace, were exploiting for their own questionable ends the legitimate concern of all Americans over the war. The Shea Bill would fill that vacuum by giving to the people a vehicle for redress of their grievances in an orderly and peaceful manner.

Then the voting machine was opened, and the green "yes" lights and red "no" lights began clicking onto the two roll-call tote boards on either side at the front of the House chamber. No running tally is kept during the two minutes of voting. But practiced eyes knew the final count would be close.

When the machine was shut off and the vote tabulated on the scoreboard, the Bill had been saved—narrowly. There were 110 votes to kill the Bill, 116 to keep it alive.

There was a mixture of jubilation and dismay at the results. Backers of the Shea Bill were elated. I wanted to make sure that their elation was not premature. So immediately following the vote I invited the Bill's supporters into my office to read them the facts of political life.

First: the Bill had received approval on just the first of the three "readings" necessary for its passage. Opponents had at least two more shots to kill the Bill in the House.

Second: the Bill had survived by just six votes. A switch of just three votes would have been enough to kill it on a tie vote.

Third: next action on the Bill in the House was set for Monday. That gave the Bill's opponents Friday, Saturday, and Sunday to work to switch votes.

I praised the backers of the Bill for the impressive work they had done in rounding up public support and endorsements for the legislation. I warned them that most of the newspapers in the state, again with the major exception of the *Boston Globe,* would probably beat the drums over the next seventy-two hours against the bill. But most importantly, I told them to get to work on the nuts and bolts of lobbying—to get on the phone and thank those legislators who had voted with them today and urge their continued support, and to draw up a realistic list of anti-votes which might be switched in favor of the Bill with a phone call and a little salesmanship.

During the weekend I received several phone calls from Representative Shea, reporting that he had been alerted to the fact that the governor's staff people were working as well, still trying to prevent the legislation from ever getting to the governor's desk.

But the efforts over the weekend by the so-called "peace people" proved to be efficient and effective. On Monday, the last-gasp attempt to kill the Bill lost by a substantial 30-vote margin, 92 for killing it, 132 against.

The real battleground was the House, the branch closest to the people. The fight for the Shea Bill had been won impressively. The ground had been broken. The Bill eventually passed the Senate easily, 33 to 6.

The final legislative step in passing a Bill in Massachusetts is called "enactment." Signatures of the House Speaker and the Senate President are required on the actual Bill as passed by the two branches, before it is sent to the governor's desk for his signature or veto.

Because the Bill originated in the House, the first "enactment" would be done by the presiding officer of the House. The Shea Bill had created such a state and national news demand, that I was urged to depart from tradition when signing the new law. Instead of the Bill's simply being signed at the Speaker's rostrum in the House Chamber, a formal signing ceremony was held in the Speaker's Office itself, something never done before. The otherwise routine act of signing or enacting a new legislative act became, in itself, a major news event because of the very nature of the Shea Bill.

It was my privilege and honor to enscribe my name first on this historic and precedent-setting piece of legislation, signifying its approval by a duly elected body of government, the Massachusetts House of Representatives. In signing the measure, I made the following statement:

For more than a decade now, American boys have been stationed in South Vietnam.

And under two Presidents — Johnson and Nixon — hundreds of thousands of those servicemen have been actively engaged in waging an open but undeclared war.

This Bill — the Shea Bill — is designed to test the constitutionality of that war. It is intended to bring about a judicial determination at the highest level as to whether the President has usurped that power delegated to Congress by the U. S. Constitution to declare war.

More broadly, this Bill is intended to reassert and reaffirm the powers and prerogatives of the legislative branch of government.

I have been advised that this Bill is legally sound. Others have counseled that the Bill may not cause a court test on the constitutionality of the Vietnam war.

Nevertheless, I believe the passage of this Bill is significant. It is significant because it represents a peaceful and orderly protest by a duly elected and broadly representative body of government.

And so today I affix my name to House Bill 5165, signifying its acceptance by the membership of the Massachusetts House of Representatives.

After enactment in the Senate, the Bill went to the governor's desk, forcing him to make the decision he had hoped to avoid. I predicted that the governor would sign the Bill, preferring to break with President Nixon and risk the alienation of Massachusetts' conservative Republican vote, rather than incur the wrath of the Commonwealth's large and vocal anti-war constituency.

The governor's great concern over the choice was illustrated in a *Boston Evening Globe* article on April 2, 1970, when it reported:

House Speaker David M. Bartley and Senate President Maurice A. Donahue vigorously supported the legislation, prompting (Governor) Sargent to note in a memorandum to President Nixon that the Bill "might be an attempt (by the Democratic-controlled Legislature) to embarrass me, a Republican governor, with you, Mr. President, my Republican leader."

On that same morning the *Boston Herald Traveler* reported that as of the previous evening an aide to the governor reported him as being still "officially undecided" on whether to sign or veto the Shea Bill.

At 2 p.m. on the afternoon of Thursday, April 2, the Governor signed the Bill and issued an enigmatic statement to the press.

"I am signing S. 5165—a measure of sincere intent, doubtful effect," he said. Further on he stated, unequivocally equivocal, "I therefore choose neither to express my own judgment, nor seek that of our attorney general, not even that of our own Supreme Judicial Court."

Those of us in the Legislature got a chuckle several days later when, his original political instincts buoyed by a substantial outpouring of favorable mail, the governor appeared on a major television network talk show and enthusiastically embraced the Shea Bill. The governor had apparently decided the measure was politically "safe." He had ample evidence to justify that conclusion.

On April 3, less than twenty-four hours after signing the Shea Bill, a "Memo to the Press" was released by the Governor's Office reporting: "The following response has been received in the Governor's Correspondence Office. Ninety-three letters and telegrams in support of the governor's signing, thirty-seven of these from out of state. Six letters and telegrams against the governor's signing, five from out of state." An up-dated memo from the governor on April 8 reported 702 telegrams and letters in favor; eighty-seven telegrams opposed to his signing.

All I could think of when I saw the governor's "Johnny come lately" support of the Bill was the many, many lonely days and nights Jim Shea had spent trying to convince somebody, anybody, that his Bill deserved support. The governor's actions reminded me of an old French saying: "There go the people. I must follow them. For I am their leader."

Since the Bill has become law I have closely followed its progress and its effect. My office has received letters from across the country. High school and college students have sought extensive informatiom for studies. Most significantly, legislators from a score of other state legislatures have contacted me as a preliminary step to filing similar legislation in their home states. Massachusetts has become the leader of another national movement.

The passage of the Shea Act is an example of the highest ideals of democracy in action. It reflected a genuine movement of the people to challenge the concept of the unlimited power of the executive branch of government. It would not have been successful were it not for the joint work of thousands of Massachusetts young people, concerned adults and their elected representatives, members of the 1970 Great and General Court of Massachusetts.

Thus, it was gratifying to read the lead editorial of the *Boston Record American* on April 8, 1970. The *Record American* is not particularly noted for "doviness" when it comes to the Vietnam war.

Yet, its editorial writers caught the real essence of what the Shea Bill was, and what its passage meant. In an editorial entitled "The System Works," the *Record American* editorial stated (in part):

> However one happens to feel about the anti-Vietnam War Bill, there is a significant something that should be stressed about how it became law in Massachusetts. Both the silent majority and the raucous minority cannot escape the fact that this most controversial measure was approved by the Legislature and signed by Governor Sargent without: one rock being thrown or window broken, one outburst of violence in the streets; one innocent bystander being injured; one Viet Cong flag being displayed; or one treasonous chant being raised by voices too smart-alecky immature to recognize the very important distinction between freedom and irresponsibility.
>
> The point is that the Bill was enacted by mature men and women who argued their differences in open debate and then acted through the orderly processes of government. They (the Shea Bill's supporters) proved . . . that democracy works–if given a chance.

I am personally pleased that this historic demonstration of responsive democracy came about first in the Massachusetts House of Representatives.

25

Diary

Elizabeth Latzer

I was born and raised in St. Louis, Missouri. My parents come from very different backgrounds. On my father's side, my grandfather was American, St. Louis-based, an executive, and politically conservative. On my mother's, he was Canadian, a farmer, academically inclined, and a populist. (He served one term in Parliament.)

I was educated in private schools in St. Louis until I came east to college. After graduating from Radcliffe in 1965 I tried graduate school, travel, and working before I settled down to learn my trade, writing.

I was active in the McCarthy campaign, both in New Hampshire and in Oregon, where I was assistant to the men who organized the canvass of Portland. I worked for a time with the Science Action Coordinating Committee, one of the groups at M.I.T. that originated the March 4 work stoppage. During the latter part of 1969 I was helping to edit their *Newsletter*.

I remember exactly the day I became acquainted with the Shea Bill. It was February 7, 1970. I had become fed up with the radical scene, the radical big shots and their tired, old radical spiels. I went to see Dick Cauchi at CPP, because he always cheers me up. There was a meeting on, but he showed me a copy of a Bill coming up for public hearing on the eleventh. I thought it was fantastic, and I decided to be there. This is the way I remember February 11 to April 2.

February 11, 1970

Sitting on the floor waiting for the hearing to begin, I started talking to the girls next to me. They were from high school in Scituate. I had my book on the background of Vietnam and showed them an irony. The SEATO Treaty is invoked to justify our actions in Vietnam, but the SEATO Treaty provides that its signatories must follow their constitutionally established procedures in carrying out its terms. Since we are in a war which the Congress has never declared, we are violating the SEATO Treaty as well as the Constitution.

Finally the hearing begins. The hall is packed. I later hear that there are about eight hundred people there. A lot of us young. The chairman is a white—correction, silver-haired—gentleman of the old school. He admonishes us: "This committee is influenced by facts and logic. It is not impressed by applause or other demonstrations of enthusiasm. If there is any noise or disruption, the hall will be cleared." We try. Any clapping is immediately shushed by the rest of the audience.

Senator Gruening speaks. He was one of only two senators to vote against the Gulf of Tonkin Resolution. He says that the President and the Secretary of State knew that the facts about the "incident" were false, that they lied to the Congress, that it was "a conspiracy at the highest level of government to hornswoggle the Congress into giving them a blank check." The chairman, Ward is his name, has to gavel us down and warn us again.

John Wells. Wonderful Georgia accent saying, "I cannot live where I live, on the Green at Lexington, I cannot live in the house I live in, the house of a man who fell on that Green, and remain a bystander." He goes on:

> In 1761 James Otis stood on the steps of the Boston State House and spoke against the unlawful arrogation of power by the British Crown in the Writs of Assistance. John Adams, who stood in the crowd that day, wrote in his diary, 'the child Independence may be said to have been born today.' Gentlemen, today we here in Massachusetts have the chance to participate in just such a rebirth of liberty. . . .

Michael Tigar takes up the same theme. Let us consider the intentions of the men who framed the Constitution. Let us consider how they apportioned the war-making power. Some said, let the President have the power. No, they decided, he would be too strong, and they had just gotten rid of a king. Then let the Senate decide; they were to be representatives of state Legislatures. No, it was finally determined, such a grave decision should only be made by the elected representatives of the people at large: the whole Congress. The President would execute a war, once it was entered into, but the decision for war or peace should not be in the hands of just one man.

I suspect my radical friends are right: I am not a radical. I *want* the system to work. I like the Constitution, though I can't say I like the social and economic system in which it operates. What was wrong with most people's enthusiasm for McCarthy was that they thought you just have to elect a good man and that's the end of your worries. "Give us the right leader and we'll move the world." But you'll never change the kind of people who get elected, or the way they act once they're in office, unless you change the people who elect them.

February 18, 1970

Rally in Fitchburg. I drove out early with Robin to take some leaflets to the woman who organized it. The woman had done the whole thing single-handedly. She had been on the phone for three days solid, calling the papers, the talk shows, people in the city. She started at 8 in the morning and went on till 10 at night. She was superb.

Shea spoke. He was unprepossessing, nervous I thought. Worth's speech is every bit as stirring as Robin said. He seems to come to the end of his pitch. He looks thoughtfully at the audience and then he says:

I want to talk to those of you who, like me, belong to an older political generation. It's easy for us to believe in the system. We've seen it work. We saw the Depression and we licked it together. We fought together in World War II and Korea. We have so many bridges to the past. But consider someone who is, say, eighteen today. When he was eleven he saw his strong, young leader shot down in a Dallas street. When he was sixteen he saw his older brothers and sisters beaten in the streets of Chicago, where they had gone to effect change within the system. He saw Martin Luther King shot down, and another Kennedy. How can he believe in democracy as we do? I think . . . perhaps . . . that there is . . . not much time left to us to prove that the system can work. Maybe it's already too late. But the burden of proof is on us. . . ."

February 21, 1970

We have begun collecting signatures for the Judiciary Committee in support of the Bill. Last weekend Robin leafleted the movie lines, but we decided a petition would be more effective. Besides we're running out of leaflets. We hit "Z" before the 5:00 showing, then I went on to

"Fantasia." We came back to "Z" before the 9:00. Almost three hundred signatures. Only a few of the radical types are so far gone they won't sign for fear the system might really do something right for a change and prove them wrong.

March 4, 1970

Hearing in Winthrop. Robin is speaking because Jim Shea can't make it. She spoke from the floor at Danvers last Sunday night and was very, very good. So they asked her to speak, as an expert on international relations. Me in my usual role of cheering extra.

Going to these hearings, I am getting a short course in constitutional law. I know what is and what is not interposition. I know that the Supreme Court decision *Georgia* v. *The Pennsylvania Railway Company* showed that a state can use its power to defend the federal rights of its citizens. I know the hierarchy of laws: Constitution, treaties, acts of Congress, state laws. . . .

March 9, 1970

Hearing in Saugus. Arranged by the high school kids who were at the one in Winthrop. Jim drives us to the hearing. We are late and he drives very fast. When he is speaking he comes across as nervous, shy, likable . . . Then he catches fire answering a question. I don't remember what he said, but it made me want to stand up and shout. I was wrong. In time he will become an orator.

March 10, 1970

In the break of the Cuba and China course, Robin comes to find me. Jim has just called to tell her the Bill is out of committee. I never thought we'd make it.

I have never been present at the making of a law before. I'm not even sure of the procedure, since I studied the Missouri constitution almost fifteen years ago. This is the second reading of the Bill. The first was yesterday when they accepted the committee report. I guess it's like the British system.

The gallery is at the back of the House. In front of me is a series of murals depicting events in Massachusetts history. Below them the Speaker's podium is flanked by a number of officials. The Clerk reads the title of each Bill as it comes up. The gallery is packed. I see the kids from Saugus, Dick, David Jackman, other familiar faces. The Speaker talks like an auctioneer—very fast. Nobody pays attention anyway. They don't bother to vote, unless someone calls for a roll call. "All those in favor say, aye." Silence. "Those opposed, nay." Silence. "The ayes have it." That way the only one who gets hoarse is the Speaker. A pause. The Speaker steps down. The number 5615 appears on the roll-call board. We are on now. Kiernan of Lowell is Ward's counterpart in the House. He is another gentleman of the old school. He is also supposed to be very powerful in the House. I hope so. His argument is strict constructionist libertarian. A citizen should have recourse to the courts at all times to find out if his rights are being violated. The rest of the speakers in favor are unremarkable—I have heard their arguments before. I am really interested in the opposition. How effective will they be? Will they answer Kiernan's arguments? The basic line of argument seems to be: (1) This is none of our business. The Congress should do something about it, not us. (2) It won't work. You are hoodwinking the voters into thinking that this Bill will somehow stop the war. (3) You are betraying our boys in Vietnam. Think of the poor boys in North Vietnamese POW camps when those slanty-eyed devils gloat over them, that Massachusetts doesn't give a damn.

This last line of reasoning (?) is best put forward by one Farrell. Is it my imagination or was he wearing a khaki-colored suit and a VFW cap? I must be embroidering on reality. He is the spitting image of one of those colonels in the TV army shows. I have a feeling he is unreal, but he isn't the only one. There are a number of them—emotional, incoherent, irrelevant. I'd find them laughable if they weren't a bit scary. Do they really represent the views of their constituencies?

The legalistic argument—it's none of our business—and the defeatist argument seem to go hand in hand. Their chief proponent is Harrison Chadwick, a desiccated New England lawyer. He seems to carry my father's legalism to the nth power, without possessing a saving sense of humor.

So far, all the young speakers have been in favor of the Bill. Now a new one gets up—McCarthy of Peabody. He begins speaking, slowly, deliberately. His brother was killed in Vietnam, but he underplays the emotion in his speech devastatingly. He denounces the bill as a political

175

move by some to repair their political images (reference to the House cut brouhaha), "it is a cruel hoax perpetrated on the youth of this Commonwealth." You can feel the votes peeling off under his attack. If I could have called down a bolt of lightning from on high I would have done it cheerfully. That man is killing us. And he's claiming to speak in my name!

Mr. Kiernan of Lowell. "For what purpose does the gentleman rise?" "Will the gentleman yield?" I expect him to answer, "Not at this time," and continue his onslaught. No, he is too honest, it seems, to use his advantage that way. He yields. Kiernan asks whether he stands accused of politicking in his support for the Bill, then reiterates his argument and asks McCarthy to answer it. The temperature of the House drops a degree or two. McCarthy can't or won't answer the argument. And he has lost the relentless flow of his rhetoric.

The Republicans are splitting over this issue. We were afraid Sargent would use his influence behind the scenes to kill it before it got to his desk. Numbers are flashing across the tally board. They are very close, only a couple of votes difference. They stop. Back to zero. They count again. Aye 116, Nay 110. We squeaked through.

There will be a reconsideration of the vote on Monday. We have to hold the line, and add to our votes. A brief huddle in the hall. I tell the kids from Saugus that they should get on to McCarthy and tell him that if he wants to speak for the youth of the Commonwealth, he should speak for them. There will be a meeting tomorrow night at Steve Worth's house to plan strategy—who we think can be moved and how.

March 14, 1970

Last night before the meeting I talked with my representative, Frye, for forty-five minutes. Poor soul, he's been deluged with phone calls urging him to change his vote. He sounds at the end of his rope. I gave him the arguments he had heard in the House and threw in the Georgia decision for clinchers. When he tried to argue that it would be very inconvenient if the war were declared illegal (a real legal hassle), I read him a lecture. Responsibility involves accepting the consequence of your actions. If we have involved ourselves in a legal hassle because of our actions in Vietnam, then we'll just have to cope with that legal hassle as best we can.

Spent the morning running off more copies of the petition we wrote yesterday. The afternoon canvassing Joy Street. Tomorrow I'll help out in Cambridge. Mary B. Newman needs convincing.

March 16, 1970

Reconsideration. Same arguments by the same speakers. A couple of amendments proposed by Belmonte of Framingham. These are primarily face-savers. Belmonte was very savage against the Bill on Thursday.

McCarthy changed his mind! He speaks in favor of the Bill, as amended. The kids got a teacher of theirs to talk to him over the weekend for something like four hours. In the end he agreed to abstain.

Mary B. Newman speaks against. She is acid, cold as her silver-blue hair. I wonder how she would jump if she were up for re-election next Fall, instead of running for secretary of state? She knows better than her constituents what is good for them. This Bill won't work. They support it in the delusion that it will end the war in Vietnam, like that! She hasn't talked to any of the people who signed *my* petition. Who does she think she represents—herself? What does she think her constituents are—idiots?

A phenomenon I have noticed while campaigning for this Bill. A number of people who by their liberal stands should be supporting it are very leery of it. I think that this is a heritage from the past. In the past "progressive" reform has always been imposed by the federal government on the unwilling states, by the executive branch on the refractory legislature. This Bill involves the legislature's taking the initiative, a state government's acting to limit federal action. Times change. What was once progressive may not always be progressive. New tools are needed to handle new problems. Like many radicals a lot of liberals suffer from historical myopia. It is no more logical to be attached to tradition because it is tradition than to oppose it for the same reason.

Our work this weekend was not in vain. At least ten reps changed their votes to Aye. Frye is among them. Illogically, I feel that my two cents were decisive. And perhaps they were. Who can say which straw broke the camel's back? The last one would never have done it if the first had not been there. It gives you a feeling of power, heady and sobering at the same time. Like when Johnson stepped out of the race. I thought, "My god, we've done it. My god, we *done* it. My god *we've* done it." You have to be careful how you use that kind of power.

March 19, 1970

The Senate is a very different setting from the House. That was brown and golden, marble-y. This white and blue, very Georgian. The House was bustling, the Senate is carpeted, calm. The galleries are on the sides and are labeled Men's and Women's, but no one enforces the segregation of sexes.

When we arrive they are discussing a Bill to allow a judge to use his discretion whether to send youthful offenders to the house of correction, rather than to the penitentiary. This is to prevent a first offender from being turned into a hardened criminal by one mistake. Ward introduces the Bill, as chairman of the Judiciary Committee. He is eloquent. I see now that he has very wavy hair, slicked down on either side, like a Twenties movie star. I have fallen for Joe Ward.

He introduces our Bill. He recounts how at first he opposed it, thinking it unconstitutional. But he was impressed by the hearing, the arguments, and the "beautiful people" who filled the hall (his words). So he thought about it carefully and decided, "Ward, you're wrong again." That's when I fell in love with him. A politician who admits that he makes mistakes! His speech lasts about half an hour and I am on the edge of my chair the whole time. I grab Robin afterwards and tell her that we have to go tomorrow and tell him that not all the beautiful people at the hearing were in the audience.

Locke of Wellesley speaks in opposition. He spoke against the previous Bill, too. The two speeches are almost indistinguishable. He'd be more effective if he weren't so vituperative. Some day the sneer will become so automatic that he'll forget to take it off when he means to be pleasant.

Mario Umana. Very volatile speaker. He has apparently not noticed that the bill has been rewritten and the time limit of sixty days dropped out. He's in favor of it anyway.

No real suspense here. The vote is 30 to 6 in our favor.

March 23, 1970

Ward offers an amendment on reconsideration. It will tighten up the legal language of the second section and provide for bringing a class suit. It also says that the first suit is to be brought in the Supreme Court as the court of primary jurisdiction (because it involves adjudication between state and federal governments?). If the court won't hear it on that basis, a suit is to be brought in the federal courts and the Supreme Court will have to hear it on appeal (because it is a question of a state law's conflicting with the Constitution).

March 26, 1970

Back in the House, to get the Senate amendment okayed. Same arguments as before. Mary B. has turned McCarthy round again, "seedooced" him from the path of virtue with an improbable suggestion that Massachusetts go in for tax-resistance in a big way. As if that would have a chance of passing!

Farrell outdoes himself: "The Four Horsemen of the Communist Apocalypse." He lists them. World public opinion. Freedom of dissent. Academic freedom. And, I think, freedom of the press. I laugh, but. . . .

April 2, 1970

We listen to radio coverage of the signing. It's over. We did it. MY GOD.

26

Tilting against Windmills

Joseph Ward

This is a brief off-the-cuff résumé of the story, as I recall it, concerning House 2396, the so-called Shea Bill, with reference to service by citizens of Massachusetts in the Vietnam theatre. Representative Jim Shea of Newton, a Democrat, young, intelligent, dedicated, a young man of tremendous promise, came to us on the Judiciary Committee to talk with us about a Bill he had filed, House 2396. It called for what would amount to a court test of the constitutionality of the Vietnam war effort; this test to be brought about by affording citizens of Massachusetts an opportunity to decline to serve in the Vietnam theatre with the protection and aid of the Commonwealth of Massachusetts in the federal court.

We first told Representative Shea in informal discussions in the committee that we felt that the Bill was a quixotic effort to tilt against windmills; that it appeared to be unconstitutional; that we could see no way that he could expect any favorable action by the Committee on such a Bill. He urged us to at least give him a full and fair hearing; we told him that we would do that with any Bill, and certainly one filed by him would be accorded every courtesy. We did this because we knew him to be dedicated and young, and a man of great sincerity; we wanted to do whatever we could to project him into the limelight of the Massachusetts political scene. We also told him that, at least, a full hearing on the Bill might bring the Vietnam war issue back into stage center, back into the dialogue of the country.

The war had been more or less shunted aside, and there was little debate on the issue because the Nixon Administration in Washington had indicated that it was headed toward a de-escalation; that it was bringing people back from Vietnam; and that our armed forces would be gradually reduced in the Southeast Asia theatre. This had lulled many people into a false sense of security, and there was little debate in the public press and in the media as a result. We felt that the debate should be brought back to stage center, because it was apparent that the Nixon Administration effort was a device to forestall debate and criticism of the Administration on the issue, and that actually they were doing very little more than the prior Administration had done about ending the hostilities in Vietnam and Southeast Asia.

The hearing was arranged for. We had been asked to conduct the hearing in the Gardner Auditorium but we said that the hearing would be held in Room 222, the usual hearing room, unless the crowd was large enough to justify our removal to the auditorium. When the day of the hearing arrived, February 11, there were hundreds of people in the corridors. Room 222 was already crowded, and so it became necessary for us to adjourn the hearing to the Gardner Auditorium, a rather large and well-equipped hall where large meetings can be held.

The meeting was attended by a tremendous number of young and dedicated citizens, all of whom expressed a sincere interest in the proceedings. The hearing was a most orderly one; we had been told that we would need additional police protection, that we should have the Capitol police on hand because we could expect a demonstration by the Black Panthers, or the Weathermen, or someone of the sort. In fact, there was no demonstration or outburst of any kind. The hearing was a most orderly and productive one.

The proponents of the Bill were first heard, and we asked Representative Shea to act as a kind of master of ceremonies, speaking for the Bill and its proponents, because it appeared that there would be many many people who would want to address the committee. Senator Ernest Gruening of Alaska led off, and told us of the trickery, as he put it, by which the Tonkin Gulf Resolution got through the national legislature, and he urged us to pass the Bill. Reverend John Wells, and Jim Shea himself, two sponsors of the Bill, spoke. Both presented a most sincere and lucid picture of what they hoped the Bill would accomplish.

They were then followed by various professors of constitutional law, from some of the nation's great law schools: Prof. Michael Tigar of U.C.L.A., Prof. Warren Schwartz of the University of Illinois, Prof. Lawrence Velvel of the University of Kansas, and, Prof. Allen Gershowitz of Harvard. Also testifying were Prof. Steve Worth of the Northeastern University Political Science Department, Prof. Ritchie Lowry, Chairman of the Sociology Department of Boston College, Professor Malik, also of Boston College's Sociology Department, and other distinguished persons.

It became quite apparent after we listened to some of the authorities on constitutional law that there might be very sound ground for believing that the Bill, if enacted, would be a constitutional enactment, and it appeared that it might very well be a proper vehicle for a challenge to the constitutionality of the Vietnam war. Besides those who testified there were many hundreds who signed petitions in favor of the Bill. My own mail was very heavy. People called my home and stopped me on the street to urge that I vote favorably on the Bill. When it became apparent that the Bill was a solid vehicle, when we saw that we might be able to determine whether indeed a President of the United States was empowered to wage what amounted to an all-out war in Southeast Asia with sacrifice of the blood and treasure of the United States without any act of Congress—when in fact the Constitution called for an act of Congress—the committee and I personally, of course, prior to the executive session of the committee, decided that we should favor the Bill.

At the executive session, it turned out that most of the other members had had the same impressions and the same changes of attitude during the hearing as I had had, and so there was a rather strong majority of the members of the committee in favor of the Bill. The Bill was thus given a favorable report, with some suggestions as to changes which we in the committee felt had to be made, if the Bill were to stand up. We then sent the Bill on the usual legislative course, first to the Ways and Means Committee. It finally reached the floor of the Senate, where it was debated at some length and acted on favorably.

It is now hoped that the attorney general of the Commonwealth, acting pursuant to the mandate and directive of the bill, will bring a class case for citizens of Massachusetts who are interested in taking advantage of the terms of the act, in the Supreme Court of the United States or in an appropriate federal court if the Supreme Court denies jurisdiction there. We hope that this issue can be tested out, that it will be found to be constitutional, and that we will re-establish the old constitutional mandate that the Congress of the United States, and only the Congress, shall declare war.

It seemed tragic, especially to us, that after such a magnificent legislative victory, Representative Shea should determine to end his own life by suicide. This came as an especially tragic blow to me, because I had looked on him as the wave of the future in Massachusetts politics. He was the kind of young man with the integrity and dedication so requisite for democracy to be a viable system of government, and to lose him is to deny democracy and our system of government in Massachusetts the kind of verve and vigor and vision and dedication so essential if our system is to survive in these trying times.

It was also, I think, a fine thing that although we in the committee looked on the Bill as being a test of the constitutionality of the war, and a device by which an individual citizen of Massachusetts in the Armed Forces could have his views tested in the court with the aid and support of the attorney general of the Commonwealth, we did achieve another desired goal. There are many cop-outs and drop-outs among our young citizens who believe that government is no longer relevant, that democracy is not working, that government is out of touch with the people, and that those in government are arrogant and contemptuous of the rights, needs, desires, hopes, and aspirations of the individual citizen.

I am confident that many young men, and yes, young women too, who attended the hearing, who followed the course of this Bill through the Legislature, saw that the government of Massachusetts as represented in its Legislature is desirous of listening to the views of all the citizens, particularly the young and alienated. I think they realized that government *can* work, and it may be that this Bill and the way it progressed through the Legislature will serve to some extent to bring the alienated young citizen back within the framework of our governmental structure, and permit him to work within that framework rather than taking to the streets, resorting to violence and other unintelligent and sometimes undemocratic approaches to the problems confronting us in Massachusetts and in America.

I think Jim Shea will be remembered, and I think when he is remembered it should be not only for the Bill itself, but for what he did for all of his contemporaries to bring home to them the essential genius of the democratic system as a device and vehicle for the government of men.

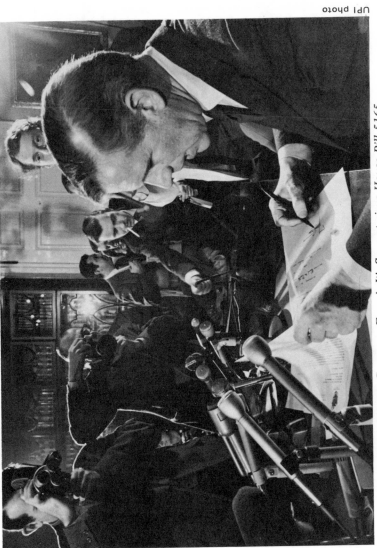

Massachusetts Governor Francis W. Sargent signs House Bill 5165.

184A

27

The End Is the Beginning

John M. Wells

The Shea-Wells Bill became law at 2:00 p.m. on April the second, 1970. Governor Francis Sargent, sitting in the press room just off his private office at the State House, signed into law the hopes and ambitions of the coalition of peace forces that had worked tirelessly to make the signing possible. This was all prior to the invasion of Cambodia and to the tragic events at Kent State.

Shortly before his death, Jim Shea made his last great speech on the steps of the State House to some twenty-five-thousand very angry people who had gathered there to protest President Nixon's Cambodian action. I was first speaker that day. I felt the anger and passion of the crowd. Here was another example of the carrying of this nation into war by presidential enactment, presidential authority, presidential fiat. There had been no consultation even with the President's own party prior to the invasion of a neutral country by the armed forces of the United States. The question was asked again and again, "Are we citizens or are we subjects?"

The tragic loss of Jim Shea as a political leader created an unfilled void in the forces that had worked for his legislation. Jim was the kind of quiet, unassuming person who listened so well, but after listening had the ability to put it all together. We felt, all of us, a great sense of personal tragedy even as we recognized the loss not only to the peace

185

movement but to all the political forces of a forward-looking bent in the Commonwealth of Massachusetts.

I will never forget the moment at his funeral when Sen. Edward Kennedy came up to me. The two of us had the opportunity to talk, but more than talk, to just suffer together. But there was still much to be done. Jim's family, Jim's friends, all those who had worked with us turned more and more to Steve Worth and to me for the formulation of plans to continue.

One of our major responsibilities was to carry on Jim's work with legislators in other states interested in filing bills like ours. Representative Andrew Stein of New York City, together with Sen. Manfred Orenstein, had introduced similar legislation with help and advice from Jim. Action had also been taken in Rhode Island by Senator Arcaro and in Pennsylvania by Rep. Norman Bersen, and subsequently by state Sen. William Cessler, who is now running for the United States Senate against Sen. Hugh Scott. A Bill was introduced in New Jersey by Rep. George Richardson; in Ohio by Rep. Thomas Hill; in Illinois by Rep. Robert Mann; and in California by Rep. John Vasconcellos, along with Rep. Bill Green and Sen. Anthony Bilenson. We helped in every instance, with the exception of Alaska, which we found out about after the fact.

All in all, "our" bill had inspired the same political issue in those states which comprise at least half the population of the United States. We feel we are on our way.

The question now comes—what is next? Under the law, as enacted in the Commonwealth of Massachusetts, the attorney general of the Commonwealth is required to bring an action in the Supreme Court of the United States, if that is possible. On July 22, 1970, the attorney general, the Hon. Robert H. Quinn, accompanied by his able assistant, Robert Condlin, went to Washington to file the case of the *Commonwealth of Massachusetts* v. *Melvin Laird.* The case is now (as I write this in early August) awaiting action by the Supreme Court and may be heard sometime after the October reopening of the highest court in the land. As a law student, and as a person who made his living practicing law for many years, I learned long ago not to predict what the court might do.

The issue raised by us and brought to the people of the Commonwealth of Massachusetts was one heavily debated by our founding fathers in Philadelphia. The issue then was whether the President should have kingly powers, among them the right to take the nation to war. This was resoundingly defeated, but today the question again presents itself: "Are we citizens or are we subjects?"

Massachusetts has acted: We think it is now time for the people of all the United States to ask that the Supreme Court rule on this issue.

It is our earnest and sincere desire that the Congress of the United States *will* reassert its rightful position as the Constitution demands that it do, that it requires that it do. We hope, too, that the Supreme Court will have the temerity to rule on this question and not duck it by saying that it is a political issue. Certainly it is a political issue—it is the most poignant political issue facing this nation at this moment.

But it is up to the people to speak. Congress listens to the people and the Supreme Court can listen to the people. To enable the people to make themselves heard, a national organization has been created in Washington, D.C., the Committee for a Constitutional Decision. Its honorary chairman is former Sen. Ernest Gruening of Alaska; three of us are the co-chairmen: Steve Worth, John Businger, and myself. In a few short weeks many nation-wide organizations have joined with us, among them: Law Students Against the War, ministers from the Unitarian-Universalist Association, SANE, Citizens for Participation Politics, National Student Association, National Council to Repeal the Draft, Americans for Democratic Action, Friends Committee on National Legislation, and other individuals from church groups and peace organizations.

Our goal is to make at least 10 million citizens co-petitioners in the case along with the state of Massachusetts. Our method is again a legal one. We are circulating for signatures briefs known as *amicus curiae*, which means "friend of the court." It reads:

> We, the undersigned, hereby petition the United States Supreme Court, to be admitted as *amicus curiae*, through our counsel, to present argument and file briefs in regard to the pending matter. We seek by constitutional judicial process a judicial determination of whether an agent of the President or of Congress is acting beyond his powers in the Indochina military action because no war has been declared pursuant to Article I, Section 8 of the Constitution.

Each brief will be signed by twenty-five persons, which would mean presenting to the Court four hundred thousand pages expressing the will of the people. It is our sincere hope that Americans throughout the nation, not just those in the states that are trying to pass a Bill similar to ours, will join us in asking that this great issue be properly resolved *through the system*, in the courts of the United States.

187

We *do* live in a grand democracy. We *do* live in a country that guarantees our rights. But for the system to be effective we must reawaken to the fact that we are citizens, not subjects, and that it is our duty and privilege to participate in our government.

Appendix

Jim Shea is gone. His chapter in this book will go unwritten. We offer here instead, the text of the Shea-Wells Bill and of two speeches made by Jim, one on April 15 and the other on May 5, 1970.

HOUSE . . . . No. 2396

By Mr. Shea of Newton (by request), petition of Mr. John M. Wells for legislation to define the rights of Massachusetts' citizens inducted or serving in the military forces of the United States.   Judiciary.

The Commonwealth of Massachusetts

In the Year One Thousand Nine Hundred and Seventy.

AN ACT DEFINING THE RIGHTS OF A CITIZEN OF THE COMMONWEALTH OF MASSACHUSETTS INDUCTED OR SERVING IN THE MILITARY FORCES OF THE UNITED STATES OF AMERICA.

Be it enacted by the Senate and House of Representatives in General Court assembled, and by the authority of the same, as follows:

No citizen of the commonwealth of Massachusetts inducted or serving in the military forces of the United States of America shall be required to serve outside the continental limits of the United States in a combat zone or where actual hostilities have been in existence for more than sixty days from the time of the commencement of said hostilities unless the Congress of the United States has by appropriate action declared under Article 1, Section 8, of the United States Constitution that a state of war exists in which the United States is involved.

SECTION 2. In the event that a citizen of this commonwealth serving in the military forces of the United States of America receives orders directing him to proceed to a combat zone or other area where actual hostilities have been in existence for more than sixty days from the time of the commencement of said hostilities, and Congress shall not have declared that a state of war exists as set forth in Section 1 above, the said citizen shall promptly give notice of such facts to the attorney general of the commonwealth and said attorney general shall, upon receipt of such notice, forthwith take the necessary and appropriate actions to implement the provisions of Section 1 above.

SECTION 3. Any area in which casualties or deaths from military or naval action have taken place within sixty days after the initial deployment of United States armed forces in such area shall be, within the terms of Section 1 above, such a combat zone.

The Text of the Wells-Shea Bill as Enacted
by the Commonwealth of Massachusetts

Chapter 174

The Commonwealth of Massachusetts

In the Year One Thousand Nine Hundred
and Seventy

An Act defining the rights of inhabitants of the Commonwealth
inducted or serving in the military forces of the United States.
*Be it enacted by the Senate and House of Representatives in General
Court assembled, and by the authority of the same, as follows:*

Section 1. No inhabitant of the Commonwealth inducted or serving
in the military forces of the United States shall be required to serve
outside the territorial limits of the United States in the conduct of
armed hostilities not an emergency and not otherwise authorized in the
powers granted to the President of the United States in Article 2,
Section 2, of the Constitution of the United States designating the
President as the Commander-in-Chief, unless such hostilities were
initially authorized or subsequently ratified by a congressional declaration of war according to the constitutionally established procedures in
Article 1, Section 8, of the Constitution of the United States.

Section 2. The attorney general shall, in the name and on behalf of
the commonwealth and on behalf of any inhabitants thereof who are
required to serve in the armed forces of the United States in violation
of section one of this act, bring an appropriate action in the Supreme
Court of the United States as the court having original jurisdiction
thereof under clause two of section 2 of Article III of the Constitution
of the United States to defend and enforce the rights of such
inhabitants and of the commonwealth under section one; but if it shall
be finally determined that such action is not one of which the Supreme
Court of the United States has original jurisdiction, then he shall bring
another such action in an appropriate inferior federal court. Any
inhabitant of the commonwealth who is required to serve in the armed
forces of the United States in violation of section one of this act may
notify the attorney general thereof, and all such inhabitants so

notifying the attorney general shall be joined as parties in such action. If such action shall be commenced hereunder in an inferior federal court, the attorney general shall take all steps necessary and within his power to obtain favorable action thereon, including a decision by the Supreme Court of the United States.

House of Representatives, April 1, 1970.
Passed to be enacted, David M. Bartley, Speaker.
In Senate, April 1, 1970.
Passed to be enacted, Maurice A. Donahue, President.
April 2, 1970.
Approved,

(s) Francis W. Sargent
Acting Governor

The Commonwealth of Massachusetts
Executive Department
State House, Boston 02133
[Seal]

April 2, 1970

The Honorable John F. X. Davoren
Secretary of the Commonwealth
State House
Boston, Massachusetts
Dear Mr. Secretary:

I, Francis W. Sargent, pursuant to the provisions of Article XLVIII of the Amendments to the Constitution, the Referendum II, Emergency Measures, hereby declare in my opinion the immediate preservation of the public convenience requires that the law being Chapter 174 of the Acts of 1970, entitled "An Act Defining the Rights of Inhabitants of the Commonwealth Inducted or Serving in the Military Forces of the United States." and the enactment of which received my approval on April 2, 1970, should take effect forthwith.

I further declare that in my opinion said law is an emergency law and the facts constituting the emergency are:

that legal proceedings under the authority of this act may be immediately initiated to produce a court decision on the rights of the inhabitants of the commonwealth inducted or serving in the military forces of the United States in the conduct of armed hostilities not authorized or ratified by a Congressional declaration of war.

Sincerely,

(s)   FRANCIS W. SARGENT

Acting Governor

Commonwealth of Massachusetts

Office of The Secretary, Boston, April 2, 1970.

I, John F. X. Davoren, Secretary of the Commonwealth, hereby certify that the accompanying statement was filed in this office by His Excellency the Acting Governor of the Commonwealth of Massachusetts at two o'clock and fifty-five minutes, P.M., on the above date, and in accordance with Article Forty-eight of the Amendments to the Constitution said chapter takes effect forthwith, being chapter one hundred and seventy-four of the acts of nineteen hundred and seventy.

(s)   John F. X. Davoren

Secretary of the Commonwealth.

Shea's Speech of April 15, 1970

Representative H. James Shea (D-Newton) today made the following statement at the April 15th Moratorium rally on the Boston Common.
We meet here again today to end the war in Southeast Asia—we have been here before. The sounds of last Fall seem distant now, and many have despaired in the long Winter of silence. Across the land, however, there is growing restlessness and frustration, and the so-called "silent majority" approval of the Nixon policies has melted as the sun has risen into Spring.

But the war goes on—we send fresh troops to the slaughter, to Laos, Cambodia, Thailand, as well as Vietnam, even as we bring home those who have survived, some injured of body; some, of spirit. War and the system give us reason to despair.

Agnew's attack on the press calls upon it to rise to defend more than ever its own right to freedom of expression as well as the rights of all of us to dissent. President Nixon has given a White House special investigator, Clark Mollenhoff, power to examine the tax returns of individual Americans. The tax returns we sweated over yesterday may be on the President's desk tomorrow.

The Nixon Administration threatens increased surveillance of so-called "subversive" groups; but how many of us will be investigated who today only dissent? In this state we have a Subversive Activities Control Board—are they out there now with us, watching, taping, photographing? Merv Griffin, a would-be well-informed Beacon Hill observer, credited Governor Sargent alone for the Wells-Shea-Worth Bill. Governor Sargent, last week, signed into law a Bill giving the Control Board new power, the power to fingerprint and photograph everyone, spectators, newsmen, or pickets, arrested for any misdemeanor during a mass demonstration, such as jaywalking or littering. This represents a radical extension of previous police power, which applied in the past only to felons. The governor owes all of us an explanation for his signature on that Bill. I wonder whether Merv Griffin would give him equal coverage for the "Sargent" Bill, if you will, authorizing "police-state" fingerprinting.

We have Attorney General Mitchell, who tries to dismantle the Constitution with a Carswell, and a President who accepts such advice and who damns the Senate for failing to blindly do his bidding.

Who can forget Mrs. Mitchell, demanding the crucifixion of Senator Fulbright—evidently *her* conception of law and order.

Vice-President Agnew and Republican House leader Gerald Ford moved toward impeachment on Justice Douglas. Yet I am sure there are many who feel, if that subject must be discussed, that there are those who more richly deserve this treatment than the Justice.

Finally, and most ominously, the Nixon Administration proposes the preventive detention of those who might in the future commit crimes. This from an administration that promised to apply the healing arts to our problems, but instead wants to isolate our so-called "problem-makers."

The President speaks out for strict constructionists on the Supreme Court, yet his attendants pursue Justice Douglas, perhaps the strongest potential opponent on the court of preventive detention because of his strict construction of the constitutional amendments concerning police powers and basic freedoms; Sen. Sam Ervin, the strict constructionist from North Carolina, comments that "preventive detention would, in effect, repeal the Fourth, Fifth, Sixth, and Eighth amendments to the United States Constitution!" Does Nixon look for justices who will ensure that our voices will be lowered? Will his strict constructionist declare, I wonder, that the Congress alone has the power to declare war?

Will his strict constructionist declare that the President alone does not have the constitutional right and power to continue the Vietnamese war in the absence of a congressional declaration as clearly required by Section 8 of Article I of the United States Constitution.

I would remind him that the logic of the Constitution is as valid today as it was in 1789—namely that when you ask a people to send their sons, and their purses, to war, you go to the people and you ask the people through their elected representatives in Congress, to participate in that most awesome judgment a sovereign state can exercise—that judgment whether to commit to war.

When I took office some sixteen months ago, I pledged to make the system perform. In the passage of the Massachusetts Vietnam Act, we made it perform for the public good. Senate Pres. Maurice Donahue has taken another step in sustaining our movement. Today, he has introduced an order in the House and Senate that would allow the Judiciary Committee to review the effects of that act. As a part of that review, we expect the committee to quickly file legislation putting the issue of an immediate withdrawal from Vietnam on the ballot in November. We should put strong pressure on the Legislature and the governor to enact that legislation.

Were President Nixon a strict constructionist or a real constitutional purist, he would have long ago extricated this nation from that flagrantly unconstitutional war in Southeast Asia as he promised in 1968.

But the President has gone unchecked in his authoritarian exercise of foreign-war policy. Unchecked by a Congress which has been untrue to its oath of office to uphold the Constitution.

Our resource is, as it was in the early fifties for those seeking the protection of constitutional rights of our black brothers and sisters, to go to the Supreme Court. Having been failed by the national executive and legislative branches, our appeal must now be to the judicial branch.

Our new Massachusetts law—requiring the attorney general on behalf of the Commonwealth as well as on behalf of Massachusetts servicemen to challenge the constitutionality of this immoral and illegal war imposing upon the legitimate political and social efforts to achieve self-determination by Southeast Asians—must be upheld by the Supreme Court.

The people of America recognize that there is something terribly wrong about the setting of a national war policy in Southeast Asia. We have been at a factual level of war in Southeast Asia for a longer period of time than it took this nation to win the double-theatered World War II.

The people know that this war is wrong. They know its cost to date defies any sane analysis of our national interest. They, in their good sense, recognize that the federal government has had its chance. They are ahead of our national politicians. The American people want peace, and they want it now.

The "silent majority" will not be silent for long, and it is not with that sick, costly misadventure in Southeast Asia. There is much to despair about—much pressure to be cautious, which means to be silent. But we know this—if we are not silent the people will rally on our side against the war.

We know this—the war will end and the system will change when, and only when, we compel it to. There is no one and nothing, when all is said, that can gag the voice of the people! We know we can direct those who run the country, or we can replace them; and they know it too.

We will continue to speak and to act—we will not let up the pressure. Our pressure for a turning around of our society. Turning around a war policy and establishing a peace policy aimed at redirecting national resources toward the social welfare needs of our people and toward the preservation of our limited and disappearing environment.

197

It will not be done with the misspent fury of violence. But neither will it be done by polite resolutions against the war.

The war will end when we take as many shrewdly and aggressively imaginative actions against the war as possible on all levels of government.

One of which is the support of candidates for state and national offices this September and November who will act with the intellect and guts we demand of them for immediate withdrawal of our troops from Southeast Asia.

Another imperative step is to generate sufficient national dialogue and pressure which will make it impossible for the Supreme Court to avoid deciding on its merits the issue raised by our new Massachusetts law challenging the constitutionality of the war in Southeast Asia.

As I leave you I suggest that this is a Spring of hope—but it must be more than that; for us it must be the Spring of our will.

Shea's Speech of May 5, 1970

Last Thursday, eight thousand American and twelve thousand South Vietnamese troops were unilaterally ordered by the President of the United States to invade Cambodia—a nation whose neutrality is respected by most countries of the world, a nation whose former leader was able to strike an internal balance between left and right, a nation with whom we have no alliance, formal or informal.

We in this country are seemingly committed to what Senator Fulbright has called "the arrogance of power." Power has a mystique of its own. Its proponents think only of satisfying their appetites.

The litany of the war in Southeast Asia is clear: It has brutalized our young, those honest and sensitive; it has destroyed our standing among nations, both friend and foe alike; it has cost us our self-respect; and it has made a mockery of our constitutional practices. We here today should all be "fellow Americans" working for a common cause: We are committed to the goal of ending the tragic United States involvement in Southeast Asia through an immediate withdrawal of all American troops.

Now we ought to ask ourselves what we can do after we leave here today. Those of us in government who have spoken to you today have our duty to make the system perform.

What we ask of you is this: (1) Support, with letters and phone calls, the resolutions of Senator Donahue and myself which would memorialize the Congress to stop the President from continuing the invasion of Cambodia, and which would place the issue of the war on the ballot in November. (2) Confront the President of the United States with the most thorough repudiation possible in November. And, in 1972, vote him out of office. (3) Put political pressure upon the Congress to order an immediate withdrawal of all American troops from Southeast Asia; and (4) sign the petition urging the Supreme Court to rule on the Shea-Wells Act on its merits.

Let us be honest with ourselves and clear to the American people. We have put aside our petty arguments and differences in search of a common goal. As we leave here today, let us not lose sight of our course. Let us remember that this must be the Spring of our will. Only then may we begin the struggle to put together the constitutional American republic whose aspirations and values are the source of our strength.